Agile SAP

Introducing Flexibility, Transparency and Speed to SAP Implementations

Agile SAP

Introducing Flexibility, Transparency and Speed to SAP Implementations

SEAN ROBSON

IT Governance Publishing

Every possible effort has been made to ensure that the information contained in this book is accurate at the time of going to press, and the publisher and the author cannot accept responsibility for any errors or omissions, however caused. Any opinions expressed in this book are those of the author, not the publisher. Websites identified are for reference only, not endorsement, and any website visits are at the reader's own risk. No responsibility for loss or damage occasioned to any person acting, or refraining from action, as a result of the material in this publication can be accepted by the publisher or the author.

Apart from any fair dealing for the purposes of research or private study, or criticism or review, as permitted under the Copyright, Designs and Patents Act 1988, this publication may only be reproduced, stored or transmitted, in any form, or by any means, with the prior permission in writing of the publisher or, in the case of reprographic reproduction, in accordance with the terms of licences issued by the Copyright Licensing Agency. Enquiries concerning reproduction outside those terms should be sent to the publisher at the following address:

IT Governance Publishing
IT Governance Limited
Unit 3, Clive Court
Bartholomew's Walk
Cambridgeshire Business Park
Ely
Cambridgeshire
CB7 4EA
United Kingdom

www.itgovernance.co.uk

First published in the United Kingdom in 2013
by IT Governance Publishing.

ISBN 978-1-84928-445-5

FOREWORD

It was in late 2009, shortly after my team finalized a major revision of SAP's ASAP methodology for implementation. One of those long days where you go from meeting to meeting, in what seems like a big blur. One meeting stood out on that day. It was a call with two SAP project managers from a Nordic organization. They were telling me about their experience delivering an SAP implementation, in a very different way from our standard approach. The team used an Agile approach, based on SCRUM methodology, to deliver additional functionality to the customer. I was intrigued, after hearing how well the project had been delivered, and that the customer estimated overall effort savings of 20%, higher engagement with business users and happy customers.

It took Jens and Klaus another five calls to explain to me all the details, before I knew that this was real, and I became convinced. We carried out further research and found several other SAP customers that had been using a time boxed, iterative based approach, with multiple releases to accelerate time to value.

Shortly after this, my team chartered a project to develop an Agile add on to ASAP methodology, to offer guidance to teams that wanted to deliver SAP projects in this alternative way. The reception of the Agile methodology at that year's SAPPHIRE and TechEd conferences was tremendous, and the new delivery approach created lots of excitement. Ever since that first phone call, we have been working with our customers to help them use the Agile implementation approach in an SAP environment.

The approach relies on proven acceleration techniques, ranging from intellectual property (IP) reuse, through to the solution demo approach with application visualization, and iterative, time boxed delivery with frequent releases to parallelization of services. In 2012, SAP took another step on its journey to embrace Agile in implementation projects. We released the first version of ASAP methodology with the Agile approach built in; thus making Agile more accessible to customers and the ecosystem.

Rewind to October 2012. I'm sitting on a bus, heading back to the hotel from TechEd Madrid show floor, where I spent the day in customer conversations about how the Agile implementation approach makes a positive impact, not only in traditional, design based implementations, but also in what we call, assemble to order projects. Projects where customers take advantage of solution and service packages, such as SAP rapid deployment solutions, and then extend the solution using iterative, time boxed build cycles. This way, customers can leverage the power of prebuilt, pretested solutions, while retaining the ability to fit the solution tightly into their environment, and deliver quickly through incremental build with frequent releases. My phone beeps and I see a tweet from Sean: "Jan, would you be willing to review my book about implementing SAP in an Agile way, with the use of lean techniques"? "Yes, of course I want to read it," I responded back quickly.

I must have gone through the book in two evenings – it is that good. Sean distills the key points, techniques and approaches of the SAP Agile implementation approach in his book. You will learn how to go about user Story Mapping, how to prepare the product backlog, understand the sprint and release planning, to actual mechanics of how to setup teams and run Agile projects in an SAP environment. But it is not a technical book, Sean balances the technical details with the people and organizational side of Agile SAP deployments, to keep everybody engaged.

You can read about SCRUM and lean in many books in the market, but translating the techniques into an SAP environment will take effort.

You can get your team jumpstarted with practical advice presented in this book, and make your SAP Agile journey easier. And of course, I recommend you all to also use the SAP's Agile ASAP methodology, as your Agile deployment roadmap.

Jan Musil

Global Lead of PM Practice, SAP Services

If you're helping an organization implement SAP's software, you've got a huge challenge ahead of you. You probably already know that.

SAP's products are purchased and implanted by most of this planet's largest and most respected corporations. They consider SAP a stable and dependable platform to operate their businesses on. But those corporations didn't get where they are by doing things just like everyone else. They've all got unique ways of operating, ways that they consider key to their success. It would be great if SAP could create software that easily supported them all. But, "one size fits all" doesn't work for swimsuits, or for software. That's where you come in.

Building on SAP's reliable platform, you've got the opportunity to tailor software that doesn't just support the business process your organization uses; you've got the opportunity to create software that people truly enjoy using, that makes their lives better. You've got an opportunity to help your organization leverage SAP to succeed. Sean's book can really help you.

Sean first reached out to me to take a closer look at what he'd written about Story Mapping. Story Mapping is the practice I gave a name to and helped to popularize. But it's a practice I've seen a great many people naturally arrive at. Story Mapping doesn't focus on collecting requirements or building backlogs. Rather, it focuses attention on the people using your system, and how they'll do so to meet their goals. Building Story Maps helps groups of people collaborate together to understand the product's big picture, and make sensible decisions together about what exactly to build. Sean's leveraged this practice to help create a blueprint. As I read Sean's work, I feel his desire to bring people together to collaborate effectively in support of creating something everyone loves. You will too.

If you're reading this book, you've got some interest in applying Agile thinking to your SAP implementation. Rest assured, you're in good company. I've had the pleasure of spending time with SAP in Walldorf, Germany. Teams there have effectively used Agile approaches for the last several years. Of course they're not alone. Today, teams in most major corporations have effectively used Agile approaches. If you're new to Agile development, or an old hand at it, this book will be a great shortcut in helping you apply an Agile delivery strategy to your SAP implementation.

But, I've got a few words of advice for you. First, remember that the term "Agile" may be a contemporary term coined in 2001, but it names a quality, and a variety of good practices, that have been around as long as software development has. The important thing to understand about Agile development is that it isn't a process. Not really. In fact, it's a call to you to pay close attention to what you're doing and how you're doing it, and to make routine corrections and improvements that keep your process working well. The goal isn't to follow an Agile process, but to take ownership of it.

If you're implementing SAP in an organization, you already understand that you're doing so because all companies don't work the same, and it'll take tailoring to make SAP fit. It should also come as no surprise that "one size fits all" doesn't work in software development processes any more than it does for business process. You'll start with a basic Agile process, and tailor it to fit your organization and use. But, you've got a head start. Sean has already done a great deal of the work for you, by describing an Agile approach tailored for SAP implementation. You'll benefit from his years of experience and hard won information.

You should use the simple rules of Agile development the way you would the rules of a team sport, such as soccer, or football as the rest of the world calls it. If we follow the rules of the game, we'll know how to effectively collaborate together on the field. But, in soccer, we know that following the rules doesn't mean we'll win the game. In soccer, we don't confuse following the rules with the skill you'll need to build with practice, and the strategies and tactics you and your team will need to win. Let your Agile process give you just enough structure to collaborate effectively. It'll be your team's job to win the game.

Lastly, don't confuse finishing on time and in budget, with winning. Soccer teams don't. If you're in software development, you're in the business of making things. For a maker, winning is making something that people like to use, and organizations get real benefit from. That benefit is the real outcome you're striving for. Great outcomes put points on the scoreboard. The software you're implementing is the output that should get you there. At risk of overstretching this metaphor, what we build is like kicking the ball around the field. The winning team isn't the one that kicks, head butts, or otherwise propels the ball around more. The winning team is the one that scores more. Keep your eye on the ball. You'll have opportunities every day to improve what gets built to maximize those outcomes, and avoid building things that won't give you a positive outcome, to kick less and score more. The challenge with outcome is that you can't measure it until things come out. If you can master the art of delivering and getting software into use incrementally, you'll get a score on the board early. It's a safer strategy then putting all your hopes on that one, big play.

If you recall that old saying: "It's not whether you win or lose, but how you play the game," well that's what we say to the losers to make them feel better. You need to focus on winning. An Agile approach can give you some simple rules of the game. But, it'll take teams of people that understand the people that will use your software, the business needs that motivate implementing it, and the technical demands of getting it built. It's this team working together that can succeed. And, it's this book that's packed with strategies and tactics that'll help you win the SAP implementation game.

Jeff Patton

Co-Founder, Comakers, _www.comakewith.us_

PREFACE

Balancing scope, budget and schedule demands in complex enterprise resource planning projects, is a significant challenge. After working with SAP projects for over 13 years, I looked for more effective ways to run them. Unfortunately, I found the methodologies changed little in that time. Most vendors and SAP customers still follow a waterfall methodology. This book argues that a new approach is needed; one that addresses stakeholder needs for greater predictability and control of project objectives.

Most non SAP projects follow "Agile" practices. Agile methods are not new – they have been tested, proven and improved since the 1990s. This book shows you how Agile techniques can be used to improve your SAP implementations. I will provide examples from my own experience of having applied two Agile approaches, Scrum and Kanban, to SAP implementations. I focus in on Scrum and Kanban because I believe that they are the best fit for SAP implementations. You will find tools in this book that you can immediately apply, whether you are planning a new SAP project, or looking to improve your existing project.

More and more teams are applying Agile concepts to their SAP projects. There is a yearly conference, SAP Projects, that has an Agile presentation track (*www.sapprojects2012.com*). These teams are showing that Agile is effective, and that it is worth your time investigating Agile concepts to improve your project's flexibility, transparency and speed. Flexibility comes in the form of being able to absorb and adapt to changes in client needs more readily. Transparency comes in inviting customers to be closely involved throughout the project, from start to finish. Speed comes by reducing wasteful activities that do not add value, increasing efficiencies in the delivery cycle, and by increasing collaboration in the team.

Given that SAP projects are delivered both in house and through consulting companies, a good methodology needs to address the concerns of both consultant and client. Agile allows us to do that. If you are an SAP customer implementing SAP on your own, then this book will show you how to improve delivery efficiencies and better control implementation costs. If you are a consultant, then this book will show you how to meet sales targets, by building long term, customer loyalty.

You likely have some concerns about using Agile in the SAP world. You may have concerns, for example, that an Agile project would not produce the right level of documentation for a complex SAP project. However, what you will find in this book is an understanding and agreement that SAP projects need documentation. Documentation is needed for estimating, resource planning and contractual obligations. You will see a different approach to documenting that improves clarity of requirements, and reduces the quantity of non value added documentation.

I do not claim to know the "only" way to implement Agile in SAP. Scrum and Kanban are, in my opinion, the best approaches to use in SAP implementations, but I acknowledge there are likely other Agile methods that would add value. In this book, I walk you through an entire Agile SAP approach, from project conception to go live.

You can choose to follow my process directly, or adapt it to your particular needs.

In 2011, SAP provided an Agile business add on to their ASAP methodology (ASAP is SAP's roadmap for implementing SAP). SAP's Agile approach is based on Scrum (*scn.sap.com/community/asap-methodology/blog/2011/05/11/asap-goes-Agile*) and ASAP 8 will contain a full integration of Agile principles to the methodology. SAP also offers formal training on how to run and implement SAP using Agile techniques.

The principles in this book are founded on what is called the "Agile manifesto." The Agile manifesto is the 2001 shared vision of 17 pioneers of Agile thinking. Following, is the manifesto for Agile software development (*www.Agilemanifesto.org*):

"We are uncovering better ways of developing software by doing it and helping others do it. Through this work we have come to value:

- **Individuals and interactions** over processes and tools
- **Working software** over comprehensive documentation
- **Customer collaboration** over contract negotiation
- **Responding to change** over following a plan.

That is, while there is value in the items on the right, we value the items on the left more."

There are 12 principles behind the Agile manifesto:

- Our highest priority is to satisfy the customer, through early and continuous delivery of valuable software.

- Welcome changing requirements, even late in development. Agile processes harness change for the customer's competitive advantage.
- Deliver working software frequently, from a couple of weeks to a couple of months, with a preference to the shorter timescale.
- Business people and developers must work together daily, throughout the project.
- Build projects around motivated individuals. Give them the environment and support they need, and trust them to get the job done.
- The most efficient and effective method of conveying information to, and within, a development team, is face to face conversation.
- Working software is the primary measure of progress.
- Agile processes promote sustainable development. The sponsors, developers and users should be able to maintain a constant pace, indefinitely.
- Continuous attention to technical excellence and good design enhances agility.
- Simplicity – the art of maximizing the amount of work not done – is essential.
- The best architectures, requirements and designs emerge from self organizing teams.
- At regular intervals, the team reflects on how to become more effective, then tunes and adjusts its behavior accordingly.

Keep these principles in mind when reading this book.

How to read this book

This book is divided according to the phases of ASAP. Given customer and vendor familiarity with ASAP, it is important that an Agile approach be overlaid onto the existing ASAP methodology. Agile gets incorrectly interpreted as a method that avoids planning, documentation and good coding practices. Although these perceptions are untrue, you may want to build Agile into your existing methodology, and inform the client that you are using "best practice" approaches to deliver value consistently and effectively.

The book discusses Scrum and Kanban techniques as they apply to SAP projects, however, it is not meant to cover all of the details of these two techniques. To understand the finer details of Scrum and Kanban, I refer the reader to three key books: Schwaber and Beedle's, Agile Software Development with Scrum, Mike Cohns', Succeeding With Agile: Software Development Using Scrum and Anderson's, Kanban: Successful Evolutionary Change for Your Technology Business. Enough information is given to get you started, and as you grow, you can refer to the above books to continually improve your approach.

This book is meant to be a guide that will provide you with the information you need to start using Agile in your SAP projects. It is short, focused and to the point. It is largely methodological in nature. My background is project management, and therefore, this book is meant to be a guide to planning and executing an SAP project in an Agile manner. I did prepare a brief appendix on custom development approaches to SAP, however, I did not try to get too far into the technical details of Agile development. My purpose is to provide you with an approach you can use to plan and structure the development and configuration work packages and teams on your project.

Chapter 2: Project Conception, is meant to provide guidance on the initial, high level planning of an SAP project. This section recognizes that the initial business case sets an expectation, and it is critical to plan and communicate in a manner that obtains customer buy in to the Agile approach. This section also discusses conditions that challenge the use of Agile in SAP projects. This information can be used to help ensure that you select the right project for your first Agile use.

Chapter 3: Project Preparation, provides Agile guidance to four key areas of infrastructure, knowledge transfer, work environment and time control.

Chapter 4: Business Blueprint, is where you really begin to see the differences and value introduced through Agile approaches. This section describes how to leverage Agile techniques to significantly reduce the length of the blueprint phase, improve the quality of the information gathered and secure client collaboration in the project.

Chapter 5: Realization, provides two key methods to implementing SAP in an Agile manner. This section is broken down into two sections: the Scrum approach and Kanban approach. Since both techniques have their place, the book covers, step by step, how to use each technique, and when best to apply them.

Chapter 6: Final Preparation, describes how this phase gets embedded into iterations of released software.

Appendix A provides practical advice on how to improve your development approach.

Preface

Books and websites referenced throughout the book are listed in the *Further Resources* section.

ABOUT THE AUTHOR

Sean Robson, MBA, PMP, CSM, has 14 years' SAP experience in project management, portfolio management, team leadership, configuration and development. A Project Management Professional and Certified ScrumMaster, with wide consulting and industry experience, Sean has managed a wide variety of SAP project types and sizes. He has worked on projects in several industries throughout North America, including manufacturing, utilities, insurance, health care, aerospace and defense, and the public sector.

ACKNOWLEDGEMENTS

I would like to thank my reviewers:

- Tom Demuyt, SAP Development Manager
- Ron Lee Latchman, PMP, Senior SAP Project Manager
- Amir Barylko, Agile Trainer and Solution Architect
- Rachel Wagner, SAP HCM Functional Consultant
- Jamie Lynn Cooke, author of *Everything You Want to Know About Agile.*

You each provided valuable comments and suggestions that helped make this book more concise.

I need to thank the Winnipeg Agile User Group, and especially, Steve Rogalsky, who taught me about Jeff Patton's Story Mapping, Ken Power's silent grouping technique and other Agile methods.

In addition, for further evaluation of my Agile SAP approach, I would like to thank Jan Musil, Jeff Patton, Michael Koegel, Norbert Klinger and Martin Fecteau. Each of you took time out of your very busy schedules to review my book and share your experiences, insights and suggestions.

I would like to thank Vicki Utting of IT Governance Publishing for being so helpful during the writing process.

Thanks also to my wife, Cherie, for her support and patience during this process.

CONTENTS

Contents

INTRODUCTION

I am hoping that you picked up this book because you are looking at a way to avoid the pitfalls of waterfall. I believe that most of us understand the issues of waterfall, but it is useful to have a brief discussion of some of the major issues, to remind us why we need to change our approach.

Most traditional projects run over budget. It is very difficult to achieve valid estimates for a complex SAP project, even at blueprint completion, so we acknowledge the difficulty during business case development. The issue with traditional approaches to projects is that there is no escape valve. The BDUF (Big Design Up Front) blueprint approach attempts to identify all possible scope and design details for a project, prior to beginning any development. Once development begins, the directive to the project is to deliver all scope identified during blueprint. This means that if the budget cap is reached before all development is done, the project has no choice but to ask for more funds.

The odds are stacked against the project. It is almost certainly guaranteed that the details identified during blueprint will need to be revisited during realization. This occurs because of the time difference between when requirements were captured, and when they were delivered. It also occurs because a client's understanding of SAP is minimal during blueprint, so they are unable to adequately express their detailed requirements upfront. It is only when testing a particular piece of functionality that the client is able to understand that requirements were missed. At this point, the team, for all purposes, must return to the blueprinting process, recapture requirements, redesign, and reconfigure or redevelop the solution. Change requests are issued for additional funds, and the result is an extension of budget and schedule.

Traditional projects are painful to schedule. They are scheduled using technical tasks, and the expectation is that all tasks will be correctly identified, scheduled and resource leveled upfront. Since most SAP projects are of several months duration, this is a massive undertaking, that requires continual updates to the plan. For this reason, traditional projects have a huge management overhead to take care of the burden of continual planning and status monitoring. As we'll learn later, Agile considers management overhead to be one of the largest sources of waste on a project.

Traditional projects are painful to participate in. Teams are often built in silos, and become competitive because of the way traditional SAP projects are structured along technical lines. As tasks run late, the downstream teams are unable to complete their work. Finger pointing results, and it is difficult to maintain a collaborative approach. Given that projects often run late, the team ends up having to multitask which further increases project stress. Overtime is common towards the end of a traditional project, as teams fight to meet critical milestone dates. The workload is intense, largely because all integration testing is left until the very end of the project.

The benefit of Agile is that if solution complexities are discovered during realization, an iterative delivery approach provides the executive with a better decision making mechanism. Using 80/20, and an assessment of value delivered to date, they can make decisions at checkpoints throughout the project, to decide where to continue spending. If schedule issues are encountered, an Agile approach allows us to deliver higher value items within budget. The client can then decide whether the remaining scope warrants additional spend. This compares to waterfall, where a client has no choice but to continue spend in order to derive value, since nothing is delivered until the end.

Although this locking in effect of waterfall can be useful in the short term to maintain sales in a vendor implementation, it can damage the potential for long term sales. Through early delivery and a collaborative team approach, you can better secure customer commitment. Given that SAP customers are continually adding modules and upgrading, a long term customer loyalty approach is more likely to gain repeat business.

CHAPTER 1: INTRODUCTION TO SCRUM AND KANBAN

This section provides an overview of Scrum and Kanban. These two approaches are considerably different, and each has their place, depending on a number of criteria. Following an overview of the two approaches, I provide you with the information you need in order to select the correct approach.

Scrum

Scrum was developed by Jeff Sutherland and Ken Schwaber in the early 1990s. It is an approach that most readers will be familiar with, because it uses time boxed iterations. When most people think of Agile, they think of dividing the project functionality into iterations of a couple of weeks, to one month. Scrum calls its iterations, "sprints," and the goal of each sprint is to build a tested, workable piece of the system, that is ready to be released to production.

Scrum uses what is called a "product backlog," to collect requirements and manage the scope. Each sprint builds a selected set of items from the backlog. A "product owner" is assigned to the project, and it is their responsibility to prioritize the backlog, to ensure that high value items are built first. Each sprint begins with a sprint planning meeting, where the product owner tells the team his preferred list of work for the sprint. The team then negotiates the sprint scope, based on their estimates. A conversation then ensues where the team gains a high level understanding of the selected backlog items, and creates an initial draft of the tasks required to complete each selected item.

A unique aspect of Scrum is its approach to teams. There are no "unique" roles in Scrum, other than developer, ScrumMaster and product owner. The ScrumMaster is responsible for helping everyone understand the rules of Scrum, and is primarily involved in removing blocks that prevent the team from getting their work completed. The product owner is responsible for defining the project vision, deliverables and priorities. Other than the ScrumMaster and product owner, all other team members are referred to as "developers." The reason behind this is to maximize collaboration within the team. The objective is for every team member to be able to perform every task on the project. This means that any one person should be able to perform requirements and design analysis, code, configure, test and write documentation. This generalization causes issues in the specialized world of SAP configuration (more on this later).

Although their recommended team sizes vary slightly, most Scrum experts agree that smaller teams perform better. Cohn cites a study of 491 projects that looked at the performance of teams varying from 1 team member up to 20 (*Succeeding with Agile: Software Development Using Scrum*). The study found that a "five to seven person team will complete an equivalently sized project in the shortest amount of time." Jeff Sutherland writes that the "team in Scrum is seven, plus or minus two people" (*Scrum Handbook*). Due to the smaller team size, Scrum has a method of coordinating projects of larger sizes and refers to this as a "Scrum of Scrums." A Scrum of Scrums involves ScrumMasters from each team meeting to coordinate work between the teams. In the Scrum of Scrum approach, planning must include careful consideration of dependencies between the teams, to help ensure that each team can proceed independently on their work as much as possible.

Another key item of Scrum concerns the notion of velocity. Scrum believes that only historical performance, or velocity, is a valid predictor of future performance. It uses the number of completed stories (features) per sprint, to estimate the team's ability to complete deliverables.

A good overview of Scrum can be found at *www.scrum.org/Portals/0/Documents/Scrum%20Guides/Sc rum_Guide.pdf*.

Kanban

Kanban has its origins in lean, and just in time, manufacturing processes. In Japanese, the term Kanban refers to a "signal card." In manufacturing, the signal card is used to inform an upstream process that more of the product is needed by the downstream process doing the signaling. A person doesn't begin any new work unless they have received a signal that more of the product is needed from their work step. Kanban was developed as a mechanism to help control scheduling of the work needed to produce a product. It serves a number of key purposes which center around visualizing work, so that producers know what needs to be produced, when it needs to be produced, and how much to produce.

David Anderson took Kanban principles and applied them to software production (*Kanban: Successful Evolutionary Change for Your Technology Business*). He found that the core principles of Kanban served well to help address issues of waterfall software production. Specifically, Anderson was able to define a Kanban approach to software that allows its users to improve throughput and reduce leadtime.

Increasing throughput is an important goal for every project manager. In software, throughput is the number of work items completed in a given time period. Another goal of software project managers is to reduce leadtime. Leadtime is very similar to duration. According to Anderson, leadtime measures the duration "from starting a feature to completing it" (*Kanban: Successful Evolutionary Change for Your Technology Business*).

By increasing throughput, the project is able to get more work done in a given time period. By decreasing leadtime, the project is able to more quickly deliver value to the customer. Anderson recommends a number of lean techniques to improve throughput and leadtime. These include, for example, reducing multitasking, addressing bottlenecks and roadblocks, and reducing waste.

We all know the perils of multitasking. Multitasking is a good way to do many things poorly. Yet on almost all projects we, as project managers, find ourselves overloading our team and asking them to get more done in less time. We try to pretend that the team has more capacity than it truly has. Once we start that method of working, it spirals, and we find that we can never catch up, because the team ends up with a stack of items in process that never seem to move to "done." It is known that people become progressively less effective and less efficient with more concurrent tasks. On a software project this is revealed in lower quality work, and an increase in unfinished work. Kanban addresses this issue by recommending we define

Work In Progress (WIP) limits for each of our work item types. A Kanban board visually shows how much work is in progress, and gives us a simple checking mechanism to ensure that the WIP limits are respected.

Kanban also provides us with a mechanism to address bottlenecks. Bottlenecks reveal themselves on a board when we see that a stack of work items has piled up at a given resource. The project's job at that point is to identify methods to relieve the bottleneck. Methods can include, for example, improving our upstream processes to ensure that work arrives in a "ready to work on" state at the bottleneck point. If our bottleneck is a programmer, then we will want to ensure, for example, that test specifications are in a good finished state, so that the programmer does not require as much back and forth communication with the analyst. Another method is to redesign the work, so that the bottleneck does not have as much work on their plate. We can, for example, have non bottleneck configurators take on some of the bottleneck configuration, so that the bottleneck resource is not as overloaded. On one project I had a bottleneck in one module, and we took careful attention to review each work item assigned to the bottleneck to determine whether another team member had the necessary knowledge to take ownership of an item.

Blocks occur when a work item is unable to move forward, typically due to a late dependent item. In SAP this often occurs between modules, or between the development and configuration team when tasks run late. Avoiding and managing blocks requires careful planning of work dependencies in the backlog. If configuration work items run late, and the development team is started too early, then the development team will spend a lot of time "blocked" by the lack of configuration. The Kanban board can be used to quickly highlight these blocks and focus the team's efforts on working to resolve the block. In many cases the development team can help with testing of configuration, in order to speed up closure of the dependent configuration work. This requires an investment in cross training, but can pay dividends later (more on this later). The development team may also have analysts who can work with the business to clarify requirements for the configurator, so that the configurator can complete work items faster.

The structure of a Kanban board helps us communicate priorities to the team. The Kanban board begins with an input queue. The input queue should be loaded with just enough work from the product backlog to keep the team busy for a week, and it should receive only the next priority items from the backlog. This ensures that the team pulls priority work into their work in progress.

Kanban uses five core properties to improve software development:

- Visualize workflow
- Limit work in progress
- Measure and manage flow
- Make process policies explicit
- Use models to recognize improvement opportunities (*Kanban: Successful Evolutionary Change for Your Technology Business*).

Later, I'll show how each of these core properties can be used to improve an SAP project.

As in Scrum, Kanban believes that historical performance is your best predictor of future performance. In Kanban, one can use throughput, a measure of completed work items per time period, and leadtime, a measure of the duration it takes to complete a work item, to predict the time it will take to complete future work items.

If applying Kanban to your project, your team can benefit through a hands on, Kanban learning experience. There are numerous games that can be used to teach teams the value of using Kanban to manage project deliverables. These games typically teach participants the importance of pulling work through the system based on capacity, rather than pushing work through based on demand. One example game is the paper airplane game (*www.shmula.com/paper-airplane-game-pull-systems-push-systems/8280/*). By actively participating in such an exercise, the team learns that throughput and leadtime can be greatly improved by carefully managing WIP.

Scrum or Kanban?

Projects can really leverage Scrum when teams are colocated. Colocation is important in Scrum, because each person is expected to be able to work on any task relevant to the sprint. Being able to work on a task with another team member, or pick up a task when it is partly finished, requires good communication amongst team members. Although Scrum has been shown to work with distributed teams, it definitely is better suited to colocation.

Scrum also works better when the tasks are more generic and require fewer specialists. At its core, Scrum aims at improving throughput, by ensuring that each team member has the skill to work on any task in the sprint. In this sense, Scrum works best in an SAP project that is more development focused. Projects that are heavy in configuration require specialists, and Scrum is not designed to accept a high number of specialists. A sprint that has high dependence on one or two specialists can experience stalls, as other members wait for the specialists to complete predecessor tasks. This can arise on a project where one module has significant configuration scope, and the project lacks sufficient capacity in that module. A sprint can stall if it is waiting on one or two team members to complete predecessor configuration. It may be possible to schedule around this configuration, however, the risk of delays is much higher on downstream tasks.

Kanban does not have any prescribed roles. It layers on top of existing methodologies and is used to optimize and improve the existing processes. It can work for distributed teams because it allows for specialist roles. Kanban is not time boxed, and does not prescribe regularly scheduled demos (although I do recommend you use demos in Kanban and schedule them "as needed," according to readiness and client needs). For these reasons, Kanban is useful for projects that have significant configuration elements and distributed teams.

CHAPTER 2: PROJECT CONCEPTION

Setting expectations

When initially defining the project approach to the sponsor, there are some key differences that should be highlighted to the client.

Working software over documentation

An Agile approach favors working software over documentation. What this really means is that we need to avoid documentation for documentation sake. In SAP, we typically create a high number of documents, and not all documents have direct value to the customer. In traditional SAP projects, customers wait a long time before seeing working software. Blueprint phases can be quite long, as the team attempts to gather all details and predict the required design. As you will see, an Agile blueprint phase can be much shorter, as we focus very critically to ensure the team works only on documentation that adds value. For new SAP customers, it is easier to present a one year project that has an Agile one month blueprint, for example. However, long time SAP customers might expect to see something like a three or four month blueprint, with the only blueprint deliverables being documentation, on a one year project. To overcome this bias, inform the client that the blueprint sign off is based on a combination of requirements documentation, and a baseline build to validate requirements (you will see that the baseline blueprint build is optional and depends on customer needs).

On a sample Agile one year project, blueprint might be planned at a reduced one or two months, depending on complexity. One month will be spent analyzing the as-is, gathering high level requirements and documenting the lean blueprint. An optional second month would be used to prepare a system demonstration, to allow the client to clarify their requirements, and the team to better understand the design. The shorter blueprint leaves more time in realization to focus on building working software, improving quality, and providing knowledge transfer to the client.

Templates should be shown to the client, since they will be much leaner than what the client may be used to. The trade off on accepting less documentation upfront, is lower costs on the project overall. Less time spent on documentation in blueprint, means less money spent on documents that will typically be read only once – at blueprint sign off. By reducing the upfront documentation, the client starts to see pay back sooner. We move more quickly into realization and through releases the client gets working software sooner. Details are captured during realization, at the time when the configuration and development take place.

This approach has several advantages for the customer. There is less risk of getting the design wrong, because the requirements gathering and design take place immediately prior to the actual build. The SAP specialist can more quickly demonstrate functionality to the client, thereby giving the client the information they need in order to clearly articulate requirements and validate the design. On traditional SAP projects, it can be months before the client sees working software and finally understands the system well enough to articulate requirements. In Agile we dramatically narrow the window between requirements collection and system demonstration.

If a company is serious about reducing the cost of the SAP implementation, they will be willing to forego lower value documentation in favor of working software. Typically, the organization's opponents of this approach are found in the Information System (IS) department. The business understands they are paying for software – not documentation. IS departments, however, place a lot of value on documentation, because they still largely believe that detailed requirements and design for a project can be finalized and approved upfront. Upon reflection, they may agree that the end result often has significant variance from the documentation. At the same time, they feel safer having the project team commit to a large blueprint document. I recall being asked by one IS systems analyst how they could approve blueprint without all the details. This was when the blueprint documentation already numbered in the hundreds of pages. I had the perception that we could have continued blueprint indefinitely, as the team struggled to document to the final level.

Ultimately, the project sponsor may need to get involved and state their acceptance of the higher level blueprint. But it is up to the project to make it clear that although the blueprint is high level, details will be captured during realization, and by delaying details, the business will not have to commit to something they do not understand. It is far too common to hear a business person lament upon seeing a configured solution that, had they had that information during blueprint, they could have more clearly given their requirement, and would not now need a change request. Delaying decisions and detailed requirements provides flexibility to the client and it reduces costs, by reducing blueprint, and reducing the number of change requests.

By focusing on upfront, detailed blueprinting, the IS department actually increases their risks. They increase the risks of building the wrong solution, and the risks of needing additional funds to complete change requests. Agile projects are, by their nature, low in risk, because of the built in flexibility. By biting off small pieces of the solution and delivering them to the customer, Agile projects confirm requirements in a controlled and effective manner.

There are a couple of key thoughts in the Agile manifesto that help to explain the reasoning behind the preference of code over documentation. The first is the broader guideline, "Working software over comprehensive documentation." The customer is typically not paying for documentation. Your customer is paying for working software.

The second key thought of the manifesto is the principle that, "the most efficient and effective method of conveying information to and within a development team is face to face conversation." In traditional SAP projects, we often have a "pitch it over the wall" approach to documentation. The configurators write the functional specifications and throw it over the wall to the developers. Obvious problems occur with this approach, because not all specifications are created equally. Statements within specifications are often open to interpretation, and require constant communication between the developer and configurator for clarification. This Agile manifesto principle simply points out what we already know – face to face communication is the most efficient and effective method to communicate requirements. In many cases, Agile suggests that we often create waste by writing something down, when it would be more efficient for us to hold a conversation.

IF THE CLIENT OR CONSULTING FIRM INSISTS ON MORE DOCUMENTATION?
There will be significant resistance in many firms to reducing the quantity of blueprint documentation. Firms view blueprint documentation as a binding contract that "fixes scope" for the remainder of the project. Fixed bid projects will use the blueprint documentation to estimate work and plan resources. It will be difficult to convince such stakeholders that valid estimates can be obtained from minimal documentation. If, ultimately, you are unable to leverage the lean blueprint documentation templates presented in this book, you can still benefit from Scrum and Kanban. You can also still benefit from Story Mapping and the use of stories to better gather requirements. (*"Stories" are essentially product features as described by the customer, and they represent the requirements for your product.*) In other words, if you, as a client or vendor, need more documentation, then the Agile approach in this book will work just as well for you.

Capacity to accept change

Agile approaches are designed with change in mind. An Agile project recognizes that the client's definition of business value will change over time, and if the project is going to deliver value, it needs to be better able to accept these changes. Change requests will arise during realization, and normally these result in antagonistic negotiations between vendor and client. An Agile project is planned incrementally, with the client and vendor collaborating throughout the project to agree on scope. It is during this ongoing planning that the client has the opportunity to incorporate changes that naturally arise, as their value proposition changes over time.

An Agile project does not attempt to lock down all scope details upfront. Scope is prioritized, so that high value scope is delivered first. If the team cannot later meet a delivery date, then low priority scope will be dropped. Many Agile projects fix resources and schedule, but leave scope negotiable. In this manner, a client can be assured that high value will be delivered until money, or time, run out. Scope, then, is far more variable on an Agile project, and change is accepted, as the client makes decisions on what constitutes value.

The conception phase can be used to clarify the change request process. Typically, a change request is considered "net new" scope. On an Agile project, the client has a prioritized list of requirements, and this provides a better opportunity to "exchange" new requirements for lower priority items. An exchange allows the sponsor to work with a fixed budget. Alternatively, as in waterfall, the client can extend the budget and schedule to accommodate the new requirement. There are often times on a traditional project when the vendor is put in the situation of having to absorb the work required, with the client feeling that it is not their fault that the solution was underestimated during blueprint. In an Agile project, the goal is customer collaboration over change request negotiation, and through constant delivery and feedback loops, an Agile project can help reduce the number of contractual battles.

Conditions that challenge Agile in ERP projects

Before getting into the uses of Agile in SAP, it is important to address the arguments against Agile in SAP. SAP itself introduced their own waterfall methodology called ASAP years ago, and even the big five SAP implementers, such as

Deloitte and Accenture, follow a similar waterfall methodology. Some argue that the nature of SAP as an "over the counter" software, requires a waterfall approach. Proponents of waterfall argue that longer blueprint sessions are required with SAP, in order to successfully understand how to configure the solution. The following will present an alternate view – one that will resonate with those who have had painful lessons attempting to lock in requirements, and avoid change orders in a typical SAP implementation lasting several months.

Customer involvement

On an Agile project, it is critical to have full time access to customers. Customers will be involved from day one in the project. At the beginning, their role is to provide and clarify requirements, but it soon becomes one of testing the solution, and providing that constant feedback mechanism. In order to be truly Agile, the project needs a customer representative, called the product owner in Scrum, who is empowered to make decisions. The traditional method of logging decisions in a decision request, escalating to the steering committee, and waiting days to weeks, will not work in an Agile project. For this reason, it is critical that the project charter clearly explains the role of the product owner in achieving success on the project.

Landscape complexity

Some ERP implementers suggest that Agile cannot be used in landscapes with too many legacy systems to integrate to the ERP. It is true that Agile involves releasing bite size pieces, and going live when replacing a central legacy system cannot be accomplished until all critical interfaces are built. However, Agile does not prescribe that each release be into the production system. In other words, when replacing a central legacy system, you can take an Agile approach that releases those bite sized pieces into a quality environment. Through this method, you still derive full benefit from the Agile approach of reducing risk, by getting constant client feedback on the build. So, although a project may not be able to "go live" until the functionality in SAP replaces the legacy system, we can still build our project with Agile methods, and continue releasing to quality until the final release.

Regulated industries

Agile methods are known for their minimal documentation, and there is an argument that deployment in regulated industries will run counter to such approaches. There are some that argue that a highly regulated industry will require detailed requirements documentation and strict acceptance processes. However, in most cases, the auditors are not looking for more documentation – rather they are expecting the project to meet strict, acceptance criteria. The key is that the criteria can be placed against a combination of software and documentation. The project will be better served by having more robust acceptance criteria documents, rather than longer, blueprint documents.

Distributed teams

It has long been known that software development proceeds more effectively and efficiently when team members are physically colocated. This does not bode well for the typical SAP implementation that outsources ABAP offshore, and has configurators located throughout the country. Global deployments, subcontractors and the preference of consultants to work from home, cause significant challenges for an Agile approach. The Agile community agrees that colocation is the one, best way to increase likelihood of success on a project.

Kanban lends itself better to the distributed team model than Scrum. This is because Kanban allows the project to be structured so that each team member is more independent than in Scrum. A Scrum project, by its nature, requires each team member to be ready to help on any task that is being performed during the sprint. Kanban, on the other hand, is overlaid on top of an existing methodology, and if your project has analysts in New York, developers in India, and testers in Indiana, you can still reap the benefits of Kanban to control WIP and manage your throughput and leadtimes.

Yet, even Scrum has methods to manage distributed teams. Jeff Sutherland, who worked with Ken Schwaber on the Scrum approach, discusses how to apply Scrum with outsourced and distributed teams in his Scrum handbook (*www.jeffsutherland.com/scrumhandbook.pdf*). Jeff recommends that a model of "distributed Scrum of Scrums" works best for distributed teams. This model is essentially one where you have multiple, independent Scrum Teams, each located in a different geographical region. A regular Scrum of Scrums is used to integrate the Scrum Teams. Work must be partitioned amongst these Scrum Teams to reduce dependencies. Jeff suggests the second best model is what he calls "totally integrated Scrums," where you have members of one Scrum Team spread geographically. Members could be working from home, or spread out across a larger area. He suggests that even in this model, daily Scrums can be used to provide "location transparency and performance characteristics similar to small colocated teams." In his handbook, Jeff discusses a project that applied the "integrated Scrums" approach successfully. In this example, Jeff provides more suggestions on how to manage distributed teams.

Jeff's real world example highlights the issues with distributed teams. Requirements documents need to be more elaborate when teams are remote. In SAP projects we find that RICEFW specifications sent to remote development teams must be far more refined and detailed than those prepared for onsite developers (RICEFW is an acronym often used to refer to the Reports, Interfaces, Conversions, Enhancements, Forms and Workflow development objects on an SAP project). This is largely due to communication difficulties and time zone differences. Clarification of a complex requirement via e-mail, or late night phone calls, adds significant overhead to a work package. One approach Jeff recommends to improve leadtime, is to write functional tests before coding. By writing functional tests prior to development, you help to reduce the downstream time it takes to close out an object. When the developer knows the test criteria in advance, he can better focus his code to align with the end test criteria. This reduces the risk of excess code that is not directly required to pass the test.

There are a number of online tools for building electronic boards to use with distributed teams. These boards provide excellent visual coverage of the ongoing work, and can be used during daily meetings to coordinate work between teams. Some of these include Agilezen, *Trello.com*, Jira greenhopper, *Targetprocess.com*, Cardmapping and *www.kanbantool.com*. You can even run a distributed project using a Kanban board built into a spreadsheet. The advantage of a packaged tool is that they have built in reports, for things like team performance and status reports. For the daily standup, a WebEx can be used for remote team members, and a projector for locals.

Whichever electronic tool is selected, it is still important to build a physical board at the main project site. If there are multiple sites, then each site should be managing their own physical board. A team member should be tasked with keeping both boards in sync on a daily basis. The value of a physical board is that it provides a physical place around which the team can plan and manage work, and a method to communicate status to non project members, without requiring additional status reports.

Fixed price contracts

Agile projects can be challenged by fixed bid contract structures. An Agile project is constructed with the assumption that software should continue to be delivered, so long as the client perceives value, and decides to fund it. A fixed price project, on the other hand, is constructed with the assumption that a fixed scope will be determined upfront, a price fixed to it, and it will all be delivered regardless. Managing a fixed price project means having to commit upfront to a large set of deliverables, with minimal knowledge of the requirements. Changes are not welcome in a fixed price project, and we build in strict change control mechanisms to manage change. Agile projects welcome changes throughout the project.

Schwaber and Beedle (*Agile Software Development with Scrum*) provide guidance on how to manage an Agile project in a fixed bid contract. They suggest constructing a preliminary product backlog, using information found in the request for proposal. The vendor should use this to demonstrate an understanding of both the requirements and perceived value, through a vendor suggested, prioritization of the backlog. The response should include an explanation of the vendor's iterative approach which would allow the client the opportunity to monitor and assess value delivery. An additional benefit of the iterative approach for the client would be the option to switch out items from the backlog if the client decided midstream that a change was desired. In addition, the vendor should point out that most customers find that 80% of the value is derived from 20% of the delivered functionality, and that with a penalty, the client could cancel the work if it concluded sufficient value had been delivered.

When we shift into project delivery, we will often find that our high level estimates do not hold for certain stories. Some stories may be so complex that they eat up time and budget that had been planned for delivery of other items. On a fixed price project, it is important to focus on delivering to the minimal specification. By avoiding bells and whistles, we can reduce the risk of overspending on particular stories. This is what the Agile manifesto refers to when it says that "Simplicity – the art of maximizing the amount of work not done – is essential." We want to continually drive home to our team that they should be focusing on delivering the minimal amount of solution necessary to pass tests. Later, I will discuss how to write acceptance tests for each story, and these tests should be used to identify the minimal work necessary to meet requirements.

One of the best resources for further information on defining and managing Agile contracts is Mike Cohn. His website, *www.mountaingoatsoftware.com/*, provides a number of downloadable presentations and information covering various contract types, including fixed price and fixed date.

Teams

There are a number of considerations when building teams for an Agile project. An Agile approach can impact team size, team composition, team tasks and team learning.

There is significant evidence that smaller teams perform better. As previously mentioned, Scrum approaches specifically call out team sizes of approximately five to nine as being ideal. Teams gel better when they are smaller. Communication flows better within a smaller team – there are fewer communication channels.

In a large SAP Agile project, you will need to organize your structure into multiple, small teams. Most SAP projects split these teams according to fit and gap. By that I mean that configurators, who manage requirements that fit with standard SAP, will be grouped according to their respective module. Developers, who manage the gap requirements that do not fit standard SAP, are set into a separate team. The developer team may be further subdivided along additional lines, such as a legacy interface team, a conversion team, and a forms/enhancement/reporting team. There are, typically, other experts that form their own teams, including infrastructure, basis and security.

It is difficult to build cohesiveness and collaboration into teams that are divided along such functional lines. Over the length of a project, each team gets more cohesive, and consequently, the project is more likely to arrive at an "us versus them" mentality. The configuration teams will compete for scarce development resources. The development resources will find it difficult to get access to configuration resources when they need requirements clarification. Each team can come to believe that the other team is not taking their unique needs into consideration. In general, communication across functional teams is inefficient.

Agile methods seek to avoid these problems, through the use of feature teams. A feature team in SAP would involve taking the concept of the SAP module team and adding in additional resources required to make it complete. This would mean, for example, allocating developers to each feature team. If the project does not have enough developer specialists, then allocate them part time to each team. Although part time allocation is not ideal, it will, at least, ensure that a given developer spends more time with respective feature teams, and gets to feel "part of the team."

In *Succeeding with Agile Software Development Using Scrum*, Cohn discusses several advantages of feature teams. For one, a feature team is more independent, so there are fewer handoffs that can delay work progress. Another key advantage is a reduced risk of rework. A traditional configuration team will batch write a number of functional specifications and pass them over the wall to developers. This has the effect of building risk into the project, because those specifications will not be validated and turned into code until much later in the project.

As Cohn mentions in his book, some component teams may be required, particularly when specialist resources, such as security, are spread too thinly. In SAP, there is less risk to a component security team, given that the security can more easily be bundled and worked on separately from the other work packages.

As mentioned earlier, Scrum stands out for its concept of the "developer." Each team member is intentionally labeled "developer," to avoid the notion of specialization. Scrum realizes that more work gets done when each team member is willing to pick up a task and go with it, regardless of whether it falls under their role description. A crossfunctional team approach means that configuration specialists, for example, should be prepared to work on tasks outside their immediate area of expertise. For example, if they know code, they may be asked to debug a program. They may be asked to help with training documentation. Essentially, you want to build an atmosphere where team members are keen to help each other out, and tackle a work item, even if it means an uncomfortable, learning curve.

In order for your teams to become effective in the Agile world, they will need training on lean and Agile principles. It is critical that you teach them the core philosophy behind ideas, such as Kaizen (continuous improvement), Kanban and Scrum. You can find excellent material to help you build your training by referring to the Poppendiecks' book, *Lean Software Development: An Agile Toolkit*. There are many Kanban and lean exercises available on the Web that you can use to provide your team with hands on understanding of the principles. Another great resource for learning principles to include in training is Jeffrey Liker's *The Toyota Way: 14 Management Principles from the World's Greatest Manufacturer*. Liker's book does an excellent job of explaining lean principles including waste, continuous flow, pull systems, work in progress limits, continuous improvement, visual control, root cause analysis, and others. Toyota represents the roots of lean thinking, and many of today's Agile principles are based on Toyota's lean approaches to manufacturing and the service industry.

Leadership

In traditional projects, the project manager is expected to actively direct the team members. This refers to all of the typical planning and control activities, such as assigning tasks, making decisions, and directing day to day work. There has been significant research to show that teams perform best when they self manage their daily work. Cohn suggests that the ScrumMaster needs to be a servant leader, rather than a pure "manager" (*Succeeding with Agile Software Development using Scrum*). In Kanban, we find that the project manager is there to help the team learn to self organize and self manage through its work load.

The new role of the project manager in Agile is to become an expert in the lean processes, as well as an expert "leader." This means the leadership aspect of the role becomes far more critical in an Agile project. Cohn suggests six attributes that make up the best ScrumMasters (and project leaders): responsible, humble, collaborative, committed, influential and knowledgeable.

An Agile leader needs to encourage the team to work out solutions to their own problems. The project manager should resist imposing his decision on every issue. This can be difficult for both the project manager, and the team, who are used to having someone to defer to. However, over time this will make for a high performing team.

High level estimating

Most vendors implementing SAP have access to a project estimating tool. This tool can be used to prepare a high level estimate of the schedule, cost and resources required to complete the project. The tools are fed with a variety of input variables that require you to identify the project scope in terms of application components, submodules and processes. Depending on the tool, it may go down to the master data level, transaction level and configuration level.

The tools will require you estimate the gap in terms of Reports, Interfaces, Conversions, Enhancements, Forms and Workflow (RICEFW). There is typically a section to identify complexity at the process and RICEFW object level. There may also be a section that identifies the organizational scope in terms of the size of the organization involved in the project. The team size and composition is normally an input, since they affect the duration and labor rates of the project. Schedule buffers may be calculated based on risk factors, such as client SAP knowledge, business process reengineering needs, and whether the project is replacing, or simply complementing, existing client systems.

These tools can be applied equally to Agile projects. Many companies now use a categorization system to classify their estimates. There are many systems, such as the ones proposed by the Project Management Institute, or class based systems borrowed primarily from the construction industry. A business case estimate might be expected to be within a range of -25% to +75%, whereas an estimate made at the end of blueprint might have an expected range of -10% to +20%. The estimating tools are sufficient to deliver an estimate within a -25 to +75 range. Later, I will discuss how excess time spent on estimating can have limited value. It makes sense, therefore, to leverage a tool to acquire an upfront estimate.

If, however, you do not have an estimating tool, there is an Agile estimating method that you can use. The approach of building a preliminary backlog can be leveraged on any project during business case preparation, to improve estimates and planning. Mike Cohn suggests that you use preliminary estimates of stories, combined with an estimate of your team's velocity (delivery speed), to calculate completion date ranges (*www.mountaingoatsoftware.com/presentations/planning-for-contract-agile-projects*). This estimating method does require estimators that have experience delivering similar software in the past.

To use Cohn's method, begin by creating a Business Process Map to identify the business processes in scope. This map represents a hierarchy that includes scenarios, processes and process steps. As much as possible, try to decompose the process steps into smaller features that are more easily estimated. Enter all of the process steps and features into a preliminary product backlog. Perform an initial fit/gap exercise to identify anticipated RICEFW (Reports, Interfaces, Conversions, Enhancements, Forms, Workflow) objects. Include these RICEFW in the preliminary backlog. Then estimate the size of each object using prior project experience, and adjust for known complexities within the current, client environment. Estimate your team's velocity (the number of objects you estimate your team can complete in a given time period), as a range between pessimistic and optimistic limits. If historical velocity information is not available, then estimate velocity based on planned resource hours adjusted for non productive time.

Next, use your velocity range to determine a range of backlog items your team would be capable of delivering within calculated timeframes. Through this effort, you can divide the backlog into won't haves, might haves and will haves. If the client has a desired go live date, then we can calculate an optimistic and pessimistic level of backlog items that we can deliver by that date. For example, suppose we have 1,200 days of estimated work in the backlog, and 10 one-month iterations to get to the fixed date. A project would need a velocity of 120 productive days per month, in order to complete the full scope. If our team has an optimistic velocity of 100 days per month, then the most we can deliver in 10 iterations is 1,000. If our pessimistic was 90 days per month, then the lower delivery limit would be 900 days. As Cohn suggests, you then need to decide what to promise the client. In our case, if we promise delivery of 1,200 days of effort, we will most likely get the contract, but will not deliver in time. If we promise 900, we will most likely complete all the work, but will not win the contract. Through this effort we can determine our level of delivery risk.

Closing

The waterfall approach requires a project where processes are well defined and repeatable, requirements are easy to capture and document, the customer can communicate clearly, and changes are rarely anticipated from start to finish of a given production cycle. The trouble is that in software these conditions rarely hold. Scope is rarely stable, and there are constant changes during the project. Agile approaches are designed to account for the variability in the software process.

CHAPTER 3: PROJECT PREPARATION

Project preparation in an Agile project has only a few differences from the waterfall approach.

An initial attempt is made at identifying the Business Process Map, master data and organizational data, reports, interfaces, conversions, enhancements, forms and workflows (RICEFW).

Key differences arise in the following deliverables: infrastructure, knowledge transfer, work environment and task tracking. In addition, the project charter needs to clarify these differences to ensure understanding between customer and project.

Infrastructure

On a typical SAP project, a sandbox is prepared for the start of blueprint, a development box is prepared for the start of realization, and a quality environment is delivered part way through realization (of course depending on project complexity, there can be parallel landscapes, Adobe® document servers, business intelligence, etc). In an Agile project, it is critical that the development instance and Solution Manager environment be ready at the start of the blueprint phase. During blueprint, you will need to demo to the client the standard SAP functionality. Many vendors have remote instances they can use to demo, however, most projects will need to configure a minimal, client based solution to help clarify requirements. Rather than lose this work in a sandbox environment, it makes sense to retain it in development and leverage it going forward. In addition, if Solution Manager is being used to store documentation, then it will need to be fully defined and ready by the start of blueprint.

Knowledge transfer

Clients often ask to have some of their own resources placed on the project for knowledge transfer. The project will need to train these resources, so that they can become productive in the Agile project. If using Scrum, you'll find it difficult to make them productive during a sprint. Scrum is crossfunctional, in that each team member is expected to be able to perform all tasks required in the sprint. This is an obvious challenge in configuration based projects, where someone requires years of experience to learn a module. Without formal SAP training, the best that can be achieved from a configuration, learning perspective is to identify Implementation Guide (IMG) activities that are low complexity, and assign those to the client, so that they gain a minimal productivity later in the project.

An Agile technique that is valuable for clients serious about configuration knowledge transfer is that of peer configuration. Mentor/apprentice relationships can be defined where an experienced configurator is paired with an inexperienced team member. Other combinations can be formed and unformed throughout the project, as required. These can include crossfunctional structures where a configurator, analyst and developer are paired to build end to end solutions that require a combination of configuration, functional specification and development. Another useful pairing is that of expert/expert pairings for members, either from the same module or different modules. Expert/expert pairings are useful when a solution is particularly complex, or requires expertise from more than one module. Pairing is particularly useful when a team member is tired or stuck.

In planning the first few project iterations, the experience level of the team members must be factored in to the expected velocity. Non SAP team members will require a minimal time before becoming productive. A team's performance will depend on the ratio of experienced to inexperienced team members.

Work environment

Whether using Scrum or Kanban, it is critical to have an open, work environment. Koch refers to this as the "XP Facilities Strategy" and provides a sample layout for a project team room (*Agile Software Development: Evaluating the Methods for Your Organization*). Schwaber and Beedle provide more information on how to define the work environment (*Agile Software Development with Scrum*). On one project, I first set out to convince the client to restructure eight cubicles, by removing the interior, cubicle walls. I had emphasized that once we entered into integration testing, we would need an open environment to improve communication between testers. The client moved quickly and had our open space set up two months before the start of integration testing. It was the time spent in this open space that made me realize the true benefit of open, working environments. The positive and collaborative communication in this open space contrasted dramatically to that found in the neighboring cubicle, project space.

FEWER INTERRUPTIONS

At the same time that you want to have an open, work environment, we need to acknowledge that team members will sometimes need to get focused time, away from interruptions. Separate project rooms, or cubicles, can be defined and reserved for this purpose. I have also found that having team members block off agreed on time slots in their calendars, helps to control the interruptions of meetings.

Task tracking

Not all Agile projects plan down to the task level. Scrum sprints plan to the task level, but the tasks are only known at the start of the sprint, and therefore are not practical for entry into a time, controlled system. Agile project plans focus on tracking deliverables (often referred to as features, or stories). It is acknowledged in Agile that finer plans often go awry due to task slippage, and resource leveling efforts at the granular task level fail when these predecessor tasks are late. To recover from slippage, you reassign team members, or shift around tasks, and the next thing you know you are back in MS Project replanning and redoing your resource leveling. Agile projects, therefore, are initially planned at high level, with details reaching out in shorter horizons. That is, the further out you plan, the less detailed your plan should be. This has implications to time control, in that resources will post time to higher level tasks.

One of the reasons you do not want time posted and planned at a detailed level in an Agile project, is that you want to build in flexibility that allows team members to work on a larger variety of tasks. Agile projects are about team members helping each other get work completed. If one team member is overloaded, then you want to have the flexibility for other team members to help get that work package unstuck. Assigning and monitoring performance at the detailed task level, works to discourage collaboration, because it sends the message that each team member should worry only about getting their own work completed. It is also difficult for them to post time to another's task if they are not assigned to it.

Another reason to not assign tasks at a detailed level is that such detailed plans often change. Agile projects refer to this management overhead as waste. Our goal is to deliver software, and not build in low value overhead. Spending hours doing resource leveling at the granular task level has little value to the client.

CHAPTER 4: BUSINESS BLUEPRINT

Introduction to the approach

The main focus of Agile blueprinting is to build an initial product backlog, and accompanying documents, representing the main requirements for the project. To help clarify requirements, a baseline system can be built to validate requirements. Note that I have labeled these steps as 'Iteration 0' and 'Iteration 1,' whereas the new ASAP 8 Agile version defines Iteration 0 as the first iteration in realization. Although the nomenclature is different, the process is essentially the same. The demo system should reflect a subset of the backlog requirements and be leveraged in the realization phase. Blueprint is neither Scrum nor Kanban. It is interactive and visual, and several new tools are introduced to help improve your requirements gathering process.

Overview

As previously mentioned, it is really in blueprint where the client begins to reap value from the Agile process. This value derives from Agile practices that help us better elicit client requirements.

Traditionally, project teams spend long hours reviewing, and sometimes building, as-is process flows. They then spend time adjusting existing processes to fit with standard SAP, and often, an even longer time adjusting standard SAP processes to fit with the as-is. This is then followed by the creation of business scenario and business process design documents – typically in Microsoft® Word® format.

These documents can get quite large, depending on the extent to which the project decides to describe the detailed requirements, and proposed configuration and development solutions. I've often found that when clients are asked to sign off on the blueprint, they have difficulty understanding the contents, because of what we often refer to as the "SAPANESE," that is found in the documents. It is well known that those of us who have worked in the SAP world, have developed our own method of communication – our own language – and if you are like me, then you have caught yourself in meetings talking in a language that the client is unable to understand.

If you download and activate the new Agile add on to ASAP, you will find that SAP is proposing a number of Agile templates – all of which are in a spreadsheet format. I particularly appreciate the use of a spreadsheet, since it prevents one from documentation overload, and focuses the analyst on being clear and concise. These templates are quite useful and they are there to be used. A lesson learned in consulting is to reuse and recycle. Never build something completely from scratch if you have already done something similar. SAP has provided a number of these accelerators and they can be used right out of the box.

The following sections walk through a proposed blueprint phase. In this approach, I propose an iteration 0, where initial requirements are gathered and high level design is defined. The approach can be used as-is, or adapted to your strength, preferences and the particular client needs.

Iteration 0 – Initial demo, requirements and architecture

Infrastructure

The technical architecture and infrastructure teams play a critical role during this iteration. As mentioned in the project preparation section, they should already have delivered a development environment to the project. However, if not, then this iteration must be used to prioritize the build of this instance. They must also use this iteration to initiate purchasing for the quality and training environments, since they will be needed near the beginning of realization.

Alternatively, more and more companies are turning to Cloud based SAP solutions. Having SAP on a Cloud can reduce the leadtime to build your SAP environments.

Initial solution demo

Before any requirements workshops, it is critical to give the customer a view of an actual live SAP system that reflects their targeted scope. The quickest manner this can be achieved is by leveraging an IDES system. IDES stands for Internet Demonstration and Evaluation System, and these systems can be accessed remotely, or installed directly at the client site for demo purposes (*http://wiki.sdn.sap.com/wiki/display/HOME/IDES*). If you are with a consulting firm, then you may have access to a remote system. A last resort is to use PowerPoint® screenshots. The idea is to give the client a sense of the target solution, and ensure you are able to better elicit requirements in a format that fits the SAP solution.

Story Mapping (aka "process workshops")

An excellent Agile technique created by Jeff Patton is Story Mapping. Story Mapping is used to gather, organize and plan a client's requirements (*www.Agileproductdesign.com/blog/the_new_backlog.html*) . You can find more information on Jeff's Story Mapping in his book titled *User Story Mapping* (*www.amazon.com/User-Story-Mapping-Jeff-Patton/dp/1449304559/ref=sr_1_1*). Story Mapping is used for more than just scoping the project. It is used for planning releases. In Agile development, it's important to deliver value incrementally, and we'll do this using stories and smaller, incremental releases. We'll plan incremental releases using a Story Map and a practise called "Slicing," to find valuable holistic releases.

Step 1 – Build the Business Process Map

SAP Story Mapping should be planned in a workshop format. Depending on the project size, the workshop may be one day, or held over several days. The first step is to guide the client through the Business Process Map. It will help if you already have a standard Business Process Map that covers the modules you will be implementing. Solution Manager contains a standard business process repository for most SAP solutions. You can also source a map from the Solution Composer tool, or SAP best practices packages. These standard maps can be used as a draft, to show the client the standard SAP process, and identify solution gaps from the standard.

The Business Process Map is used to identify scope for each SAP component or module at the business scenario, process and process step level. Each of these levels is a method of drilling down into a given business area, to identify the relevant SAP functionality for the requirements of that business. Typically, a process step gets solutioned by a transaction, a RICEFW, or a combination, but it can also be solutioned by a manual step, or a step outside of SAP (the related system action is sometimes referred to as an "activity"). Processes and their process steps are often drawn as process flows, with swim lanes being added to represent the assigned roles for each step.

If it has not already been done, you will need to expand the scenarios into their processes and process steps (scenarios and processes are often initially gathered during business case formulation, and/or project preparation phases, since they are needed in scoping the project). Once you have the processes, you are ready to identify the client's process steps. Using the standard SAP process steps as a straw man, you will now revise and add in client specific steps.

VANILLA SAP

Many clients state that they want "vanilla SAP," but once they see the standard Business Process Map, they immediately find they need to revise, add or remove processes. Since each process step in a standard Business Process Map normally equates to a standard transaction, diverging from the standard Business Process Map can mean RICEFW customization, or complex, configuration work. The mapping exercise is your first opportunity to determine whether standard processes will meet the client requirements. If the sponsor's project goal is to implement vanilla SAP, then you will want to use the standard Business Process Map to initiate discussions on where the business may need to change its processes to "fit" standard SAP.

Workforce Management	Workforce Benefits Administration	Workforce Time Management	Workforce Payroll Administration
• Maintain company organizational structures	• Benefits enrollment and termination	• Time entry	• Payroll and post payroll processing
• Creating organizational units, jobs and positions	• New hire enrollment into benefits	• Manual time entry – attendances	• Maintain master data and time data
• Maintaining organizational units, jobs and positions	• Open enrollment processing	• Manual time entry – absences	• Run payroll
• Organization and staffing changes	• Maintaining employee elections in each benefit plan	• Manual time entry – weekly screen	• Run FI/CO posting and third party remittance
• New hire/rehire administration	• Map beneficiaries and dependents to specific plans	• Cross application timesheet entry and release	• Payment management
• New hire	• Print confirmation or enrollment statements.	• Time processing – cross application timesheet (CATS)	• Off cycle payroll
• Rehire	• Terminate benefit plans upon the employee's departure	• Review and approve the employee's time	• Payroll journal reporting
• Activate non employee	• Benefits administration	• Transfer the time to the various SAP modules	• Retroactive payroll processing
• Reactivate non employee	• Mass generation of adjustment reasons	• Time administration	• Set controls for retroactive changes
• Employee terminations	• Group enrollment into specified benefit plans	• Employee quota overview	• Change payroll relevant master data
• Employee separation	• Monitoring of employee elections in each benefit plan	• Absence quota report	• Execute retroactive payroll
• Employee retirement	• Validating employee elections	• Creating quotas manually	• Off cycle payroll processing
• Deactivate non employee	• Adjusting employee's data	• Quota corrections	• Process employee off cycle payroll
• Leave of absence (LOA) processing		• Time quota compensation	• Run payroll
• Leave of absence – active status		• Time evaluation processing	• Execute a correction payroll
• Leave of absence – inactive status		• Process time evaluation	• Process payroll data for a manual check
• Return to work from active		• View time cluster	• View an employee's payroll history
• Return to work from inactive		• View time results	• Replace payments
• Employee transfer administration		• Time management pool	• Reverse payments
• Change in position		• Time statement form	• Adjust W2 data
• Change in pay			• Period end closing for HCM
• Maintain employee information			• Day end closing
• Creating employee master data			• Month end closing
• Maintaining employee master data			• Quarterly closing
			• Year end closing

Figure 1: Human capital management Business Process Map

The Business Process Map shown in Figure 1 is adapted from SAP's Best Practices for Human Capital Management for the United States solution scope (*http://help.sap.com/saap/sap_bp/HCM_ERP605_US/html/index.htm*).

The Business Process Map is an excellent, and time proven method, of capturing process scope for SAP projects. It also maps to the Solution Manager process hierarchy and can, in fact, be initially built in Solution Manager then worked through with a customer to refine it.

DIFFERENT WAYS TO BUILD THE BUSINESS PROCESS MAP

In many cases, a Business Process Map will be maintained in a spreadsheet format. However, an alternative method is to build it out with the client, using index cards or sticky notes. A valuable lesson from Agile is the more interaction you create between the customer and your team members, the better your outcome from the effort. Simply having the customer and team stand up and create the map together, is far more effective than our typical method of "presenter-audience." The "presenter-audience" method, where one person sits at the keyboard, creates far too little audience engagement. Because of the effectiveness of a simple technique of using sticky notes, you will find further examples throughout this book.

Step 2 – Building the Story Map and identifying stories

We will now leverage our Business Process Map to identify the customer's requirements. On a traditional project, we would normally begin to document detailed requirements and design decisions in business process design documents. In an Agile project, we want to avoid what is called BDUF – Big Design Up Front. We leave the detailed decisions as late as possible, so that we avoid all of the issues related with BDUF, discussed earlier in the book. We create "lean" blueprint documents, but our main blueprint activity is to identify what are called "stories." Avoiding detail upfront isn't the same as avoiding thinking upfront, and certainly not the same as avoiding getting the big picture upfront. A blueprint built with a Story Map gives us a big picture and an early look at the whole solution. We'll use this to help us identify the riskiest parts and most valuable parts early, because if we're going to progressively get into the details, it's those risky and valuable details that are the best place to start.

Mike Cohn defines a story as "functionality that is valuable to either a user or purchaser of a system or software" (*Agile Estimating and Planning*). Most importantly, a story is written in the language of the business person, by the business person. A story is a promise to the customer that when you are ready to work on the story, you will get back together, converse and gather the details.

You will need both your team, and the customer, to understand that a story is not meant to capture all details. It is not a detailed requirements specification. The purpose of a story is to document, high level, the requirement, but not to delve into too many details. A story is typically collected on a three by five card, or a sticky note. The size of the card, or note, restricts someone from documenting too many details. Details must be saved for when the story is ready to be developed. The only thing that needs to be documented for a story, initially, is the story description and its acceptance criteria. Acceptance criteria are discussed in detail later, but in short, they define conditions that the story must meet before being considered complete.

As Cohn suggests, a story should ideally be documented in the format of "As a [type of user] I want [some feature] so that [some benefit is received]." By identifying the type of user, we ensure that we keep the developer focused on the customer. The feature section represents the high level requirement. Traditionally, we have written requirements as "the system shall" statements. You want to avoid that because of the many errors it introduces. Writing clear and concise requirement statements requires considerable skill. Unclear requirements statements lead to games of interpretation between the analyst and the user during realization. By stating the requirement in terms of a user activity, you ensure that the user will always understand the requirement. You do not always need to define the benefit, however, it can be useful in helping to prioritize the story. An example story is "As a payroll administrator I want to be able to pay someone outside of a regular pay run, so that I can process special payments."

We use a Story Map to identify stories. The first iteration of the Story Map serves as the client's focal point for brainstorming stories at the process step level. We take the Business Process Map and transform it into a view that fits the design of a Story Map.

A Story Map layout can be created with sticky notes on a wall, or with index cards on tables. They can become quite large for some projects, and it is important to give some thought as to location, since the Story Map will ideally remain visible throughout the project. Alternatively, the Story Map can be built in an electronic tool. There a number of online tools that can be used, such as *Cardmapping.com*, or you can use Microsoft® Excel® or Visio®. If you anticipate that your Story Map will be too large to manage with physical cards or sticky notes, then you will want to consider collecting it electronically. Large SAP projects can have hundreds of stories, and it can be difficult to manage these in a Story Map. One trick is to "downsize" the size of the cards by printing business card size cutouts for each story, and to build a map using these smaller size cards on a large enough table workspace.

Another method of reducing the initial size of the Story Map is to combine smaller stories into epics and themes. Epics are simply large stories. In Agile, a story is considered large when it takes longer than 10 days. For example, at this point in the project you may find out that you need to configure healthcare plans. Your team may tell you that designing, configuring and testing healthcare plans will take approximately 30 days. If you do not plan on starting work on healthcare plans for another two months, then you do not necessarily have to break this epic into smaller stories until closer to the start date. Similar to epics, themes group together related stories. "By aggregating some stories into themes and writing some stories as epics, a team is able to reduce the effort they'll spend on estimating" (Cohn, *Agile Estimating and Planning*).

Online mapping has the downside of reducing the collaborative effect created when users write stories on physical cards and build a physical, Story Map. If at all possible, it is best to colocate the team members and build the Story Map together.

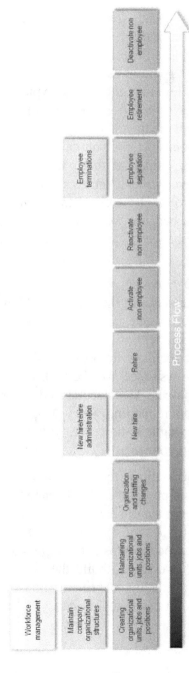

Figure 2: Sampling of Business Process Map items converted to a Story Map

To create the Story Map, transfer each Business Process Map item to an index card or sticky note. Figure 2 shows a section of the Business Process Map converted into a Story Map view. You will notice that the steps for each process are laid out from left to right, in the typical sequence in which they are performed (reserve a room with sufficient space for the full map to be built in sequence). In sequencing the process steps, you can use SAP's standard process flows as a guide. At this point, you are building what is often referred to as a "straw man." A straw man is our best guess as to what the client may want or need. We call it a straw man because we want our customer to know that we intend to change it. It is a draft built for discussion purposes.

We now need the client to rearrange the sticky notes, so that the process steps are in the order in which they would most often be performed in their business. This is an alternative to documenting flows in a process flow diagramming tool, such as Microsoft® Visio® (this does not rule out process flows – see note below). Figure 3 shows a sampling of the process steps sequenced in order of time (for simplicity, the remaining Story Map figures do not show levels 1 through 3, however, you would normally keep these levels in your map).

Just as in any process flow, there are numerous inputs and outputs to any given process. In this linear Story Map view, we want to document the business process flow sequence in the manner in which it "most often" appears. The purpose of sequencing the process steps is to help us understand the sequence in which we should build the system. Later, you will document, in a lean blueprint template, the specific inputs and outputs for each process step.

Figure 3: Story Map sequenced processed steps

DO WE STILL NEED PROCESS FLOWS?

The Story Map helps the business understand the processes. It can replace actual process flows, or complement them. It structures, from left to right, the flow of the business process. It further shows all detailed activities (stories) that the business performs. But some process steps are so complex that they can benefit from a process flow that shows decisions, entry and exit points. You definitely want to use all tools at your disposal to ensure that you capture an accurate picture of the business processes. If process flows help your client represent their business, then you will definitely want to leverage them.

Once you have your process steps in sequence, you can begin to disaggregate the process steps into smaller stories. These stories will later be moved into your product backlog which can be maintained in a spreadsheet format (*see the section title "Product Backlog"*). The process of gathering stories is a very dynamic activity, involving the team members and the business. The exercise is used to identify project scope, proper build sequence, and capture any additional gaps.

The feature portion of the story is used to identify business tasks. For each process step you want to focus on, ask your client the types of tasks they perform. Tasks will usually come with an action verb. Have your team and customer work through each process step to break them down into individual business tasks. For example, when hiring an employee, there are a number of tasks that a client will perform. Tasks can include maintaining the employee's basic data, assigning the employee to a position, entering banking information, entering education information, etc. Again, notice that each task begins with a verb to describe the action taken by the user. Each task should be complete, in and of itself, meaning that the task should have an objective that gets realized upon its completion. Write the tasks on the cards or sticky notes in a short form that includes the verb and the subject, and place them on the wall, or table, beneath their respective process steps.

WHAT TO INCLUDE ON A CARD

The full story statement involves identifying the user, the feature and the benefit. You can record all three items on the card, or simply record the feature, and enter the user and benefit into the product backlog. Patton suggests two additional items you may want to record on each card: the frequency that the task is performed (high, medium, low, daily, weekly, etc.) and an assessment of value (high, medium, low). Frequency and value assessments can help the client better understand where to place the cards in the map on the vertical axis.

If the client proposes a story that your team feels is quite complex, then you have what Agile calls an "epic." An epic is simply a large story that will need to be broken down later, when the team is ready to work on it. The client may also think of a number of tasks that are related. Rather than list out separate stories for each related task, you can group them into one story called a "theme." Most Agile projects delay breaking down epics and themes until the iteration, when the stories will be worked on. This practice can be quite useful for estimating purposes, and to better control the time it takes to identify stories upfront (more on estimating later). However, if your team feels they need more information on the epic or theme, in order to identify gaps, or perform a better estimate, then you should take time to break them down now.

The activity of collecting these tasks can be done in smaller brainstorming groups. Assign a collection of process steps to various groups, and ask them to brainstorm the tasks involved in each process step. Have one of the team members take notes, to capture details on acceptance tests as they arise (acceptance tests will be covered shortly). Have each team post their sticky notes in order of priority and value to the business, under their respective process step.

When assigning priorities, be sure to remind your client and project team of the business case objectives of the project. The value driver for each story should be clearly understood, and the final build of the solution should demonstrate that value was realized.

Jeff makes a valid point that in prioritization of deliverables it is important to consider the frequency the tasks occur. More frequent tasks will normally be prioritized more highly, since the business will need their functionality to complete daily work. However, it is important to consider that some tasks will be critical, even if they are infrequent in occurrence. These infrequent tasks should be considered critical if deemed so by the business. The stakeholders will be able to identify these tasks for you during the Story Mapping exercise.

Figure 4 shows the Story Map with the sequenced tasks.

To manage dependencies between stories, ensure that the prioritization effort builds in core pieces of functionality first. Work with the customer to align their business priorities to the sequence in which SAP functionality is best built.

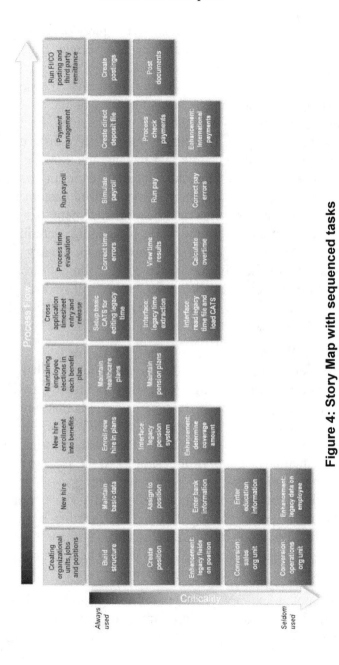

Figure 4: Story Map with sequenced tasks

You will note that not all items in Figure 4 are user stories. RICEFW need not be entered in story format, because they do not always meet the definition of a story in terms of being a task that the end user performs. Interfaces, for example, occur outside the boundaries of the system, and are transparent to the end user. Conversions are run only during the project. By identifying RICEFW differently, we can more easily schedule and manage the work, given that it is performed by the development team. In the sample Story Map, there is an enhancement to add custom fields to the position. There is another enhancement designed to improve employee reporting, by adding certain legacy fields to the employee. A downstream, legacy pension system will need to receive pension enrollment information, and an upstream, timekeeping system will need to transfer time data through to SAP. These gaps get identified through conversations that take place while building the Story Map.

RICEFW stories can, at first, be defined in the same manner as they are on traditional projects. That is, you should identify one, high level story, to identify a RICEFW object uniquely. The difference in Agile is that you need to continue to break the high level RICEFW story down into stories of a smaller size. You want smaller stories because the smaller the story, the simpler it is for the team to analyze, build and test. This meets our goal of delivering working software early and continuously. The sample Story Map shows that the legacy time interface has been broken down into three manageable stories. The parent story of "Legacy Time Interface" can be tracked in the product backlog and linked to the child stories.

As another example, conversion stories can be broken down into smaller stories that are built and delivered "as needed" and in small packages. Rather than spend weeks, or months, on an employee data extraction for thousands of employees, you can first define a story that converts data for one department. This allows the team to bite off pieces of the conversion effort, and ensures early delivery of actual converted data for test purposes. The larger story "Convert Employee data" gets broken down into smaller conversion packages that can be built and delivered on an as needed basis.

Returning to the story board, you see that stories have been entered into their vertical columns in priority sequence. This sequencing represents the highest to lowest value items as perceived by the customer. These priorities will be used in helping to plan the releases. Planning releases requires significant SAP experience, since there are many dependencies to consider. What is important though, is that releases be designed with the user's needs in mind. Each release must contain something valuable from an end user perspective. This becomes important when considering RICEFW objects.

Traditionally, we sequence realization, so that first a baseline configuration is built. We then add on additional configuration and RICEFW objects. There are two primary issues with this approach. The first has to do with the lack of end user focus. The purpose of Agile projects is to return the focus to the user goals and objectives. By being user story centric, we ensure that we are continually delivering value to the customer. Another issue with this approach is that it assumes that the RICEFW objects can be smoothly integrated into the baseline configuration. Unfortunately, this is rarely the case, particularly with interfaces. A complex, system landscape with aging, legacy systems will have requirements that are difficult to understand, and often drive changes to configuration.

On one project, the customer informed me that no one had documented the aging, legacy interfaces, and no one could remember what exactly had been coded. We had to bring in experts who could read the legacy system's code, in order to understand requirements. As each legacy interface was analyzed, it was found that rework was needed in the configuration. To avoid these issues, you need to ensure that releases are constructed with the business process in mind. We need to be building release ready systems in each release. In our example, the client has a legacy system that collects time data from terminals. This time data needs to be imported to the SAP CAT2 transaction. Delivering the CAT2 transaction without the interface, will have no value to the customer. The two must be developed together. Later, in realization, these two stories will be scheduled and analyzed together. This will ensure that the design takes all requirements into consideration, and reduces the risk of rework.

It is now time for the client and project team to identify useful releases. Each release should contain a cohesive set of user stories that hold meaning to the customer. Anderson refers to the "minimal marketable release" (MMR), which means identifying the minimal set of features that will hold value to the customer, and be meaningful enough to justify delivery costs (*Kanban: Successful Evolutionary Change for Your Technology Business*).

Release planning

Overview

There are a number of key steps involved in this activity, with the primary objective of identifying methods of breaking up the solution into incremental, releasable and meaningful sections, delivered every three to six months. The ideal is to transport tested code for each release to your quality environment, conduct integration testing and a release specific, cutover rehearsal, then cutover to production.

Consider the difficulties of a typical, one year SAP project. The team configures, develops and unit tests over a period of four to five months. Once all functionality has been unit tested, the integration test team prepares to test the end to end functionality in the quality environment. Many projects see integration testing as holding some sort of contingency. That is, if the project can cut anywhere, they are most likely to cut short the integration testing. If test cycles are too short, the integration test team will have difficulty getting through all test scenarios, resolving defects and completing the cycles on time, prior to cutover.

At the same time, the cutover team is working hard to plan the detailed steps needed to cutover over a huge system in one "big bang" approach. This is not an easy task, and we hold cutover rehearsals to reduce risk. These cutover rehearsals are time consuming, and given the pressures to hit a go live date, the risk going live with unknown defects is high. Stabilization periods in a complex SAP implementation can run for weeks, and even months, as the client and the sustainment team work to resolve issues.

For these reasons, the Agile approaches do not recommend big bang implementations. One of the 12 principles of the Agile manifesto is to "deliver working software frequently, from a couple of weeks to a couple of months, with a preference to the shorter timescale." The effort to perform integration testing and cutover gets progressively easier as you reduce the scope of the cutover. You can reduce scope by releasing more frequently. This then becomes the goal of release planning in an SAP project.

There are aspects to some SAP projects that make frequent release to a production environment difficult. For example, clients that have many complex system landscapes may be unable to release to production without having the applicable interfaces in place. Other clients may have complex production systems, and be hesitant to perform frequent cutovers, due to the disruption to the existing business.

If you find that you are unable to perform your release all the way to production, then your next best option is to release to the quality environment. Through this effort, you can still iterate through your integration testing and cutover rehearsals for each release, and reduce the risk of the big bang effort at final go live.

The key point here is that on an Agile SAP project, you do not have one realization – final preparation phase. You iterate through several realization – final preparations, until the client feels that either enough of the backlog has been completed for them to go live, or the budget or time constraints have been reached.

The product backlog

The product backlog contains the full list of accepted requirements for the project, in a list format. Since requirements are collected in story format, they form the primary contents of the product backlog. The backlog can be maintained in a spreadsheet. A sample backlog, followed by a field description, are shown on the following pages.

One very important distinction about the product backlog, is that it must be the one, golden source for the project scope. The Story Map provides a visual of the project scope, but the product backlog represents the one source of truth, since it will be continually updated with any new, or revised, stories. One of the main drawbacks of the typical SAP project, is that one must read through several documents and sources in order to understand the scope of the project. One of the most valuable outputs of the Agile approach, is the notion of maintaining "one source" for the project scope. That means that this backlog must contain client requirements, technical requirements, RICEFW objects, infrastructure, and anything else of significance to the project. The backlog can even be used to track major defects.

STORY ID	PROCESS GROUP	PROCESS	PROCESS STEP (PARENT STORY)	STORY	STORY ACCEPTANCE CRITERIA
S_0001	Workforce benefits administration	Benefits administration	Enroll employee(s) in benefits	Able to maintain healthcare plans for employees	Two policies for separate employee types; four styles within each policy; dependent age restrictions
S_0002	Workforce benefits administration	Benefits administration	Enroll employee(s) in benefits	Able to maintain healthcare plans for retirees	
S_0003	Workforce benefits administration	Benefits administration	Enroll employee(s) in benefits	Able to maintain life plans for employees	
S_0004	Workforce benefits administration	Benefits administration	Enroll employee(s) in benefits	Able to maintain life plans for retirees	13 policies with five grandfathered, two closed, six active
S_0005	Workforce benefits administration	Benefits administration	Enroll employee(s) in benefits	Able to maintain dental plans for employees	

S_0006	Workforce benefits administration	Benefits administration	Enroll employee(s) in benefits	Able to maintain company match RRSP plans for employees	
S_0007	Workforce benefits administration	Benefits administration	Enroll employee(s) in benefits	Able to maintain company pension plans for employees	
S_0008	Workforce benefits administration	Benefits administration	Enroll employee(s) in benefits	Able to enroll new hire in their eligible plans	Offering changes depending on the adjustment reason
S_0009	Workforce benefits administration	Benefits administration	Enroll employee(s) in benefits	Able to control enrollment for new hire	Able to change benefits for one month following initial hiring; after one month, the system prevents change of plans for a new hire
S_0010	Workforce benefits administration	Benefits administration	Record adjustment reasons for why a benefit was changed	Able to record an adjustment reason for why a benefit is being changed	Can maintain the following reasons, hire, family status change, job change, annual reenrollment

Figure 5: Sample product backlog showing high level acceptance criteria

FIELD NAME	DESCRIPTION
Story ID	Each story should be identified by a unique ID.
Process group	Identify the process group from the Business Process Map under which the story was collected.
Process	Identify the process from the Business Process Map under which the story was collected.
Process step (parent story)	Identify the process step from the Business Process Map under which the story was collected.
Story acceptance criteria	The acceptance criteria found in the product backlog is at a high level and is used in sizing the work. These can be entered in a list format and contain criteria that must be met in order to satisfy the story. The criteria are later expanded on during realization, when ready to work on the story.
User	Record the user associated with the story, if known.
Benefit/value of story	Record the benefit provided by the customer.
Notes/dependencies/prerequisites	Enter any notes or comments collected, either during the Story Mapping exercise, or later. You should also make note of any key dependencies and prerequisites.
Priority	The priority should be identified using your preferred prioritization method (for example, must have, nice to have, etc).

Priority sequence	In Scrum, the product owner is required to maintain a sequential ordering of the backlog. Each requirement must have its own unique number. Kanban is less prescriptive and allows for last minute prioritization when filling the input queue.
Rough effort estimation	Record the story points or ideal days estimate. Note though, that the ideal is to have each story similarly sized (as close to five as possible is ideal) as this will facilitate work planning.
Release	Record the release to which the story is assigned.
Sprint	If using Scrum, then record the sprint in which the story will be assigned.
Status	Record whether the story is new, in process or done.

Figure 6: Product backlog fields

Strategy

There are two strategic methods of approaching the releases. A functionality driven approach involves working with the client to identify the stories required to produce the first valuable release. A timeline, or budget driven approach, reviews the effort estimates in the backlog, to identify the number of requirements that can be fulfilled within a given schedule or budget. In most cases, your strategy will involve a hybrid of the two approaches.

Slicing

Agile author, Jeff Patton, discusses slicing as a technique used to break the larger project scope into deliverable sections (*www.Agileproductdesign.com/writing/how_you_slice_it.pdf*). Jeff's approach is adaptable to an SAP project because of its business, process driven approach to identifying dividing points in the releases. Note that you may come across other Agile terms, such as sashimi, that refer to the same approach of delivering slices of the full product.

Jeff recommends looking at your Story Map from left to right, until you encounter a logical break in the workflow. As he suggests, breaks often occur when there is a role change. If your client identified users for each story, you can leverage these to help identify these breaks. Once you have selected a logical set of process steps, you can identify the smallest set of features that would hold value to the client. Each release should consist of the set of stories that your team can deliver in the desired timeframe for a release.

You will want to review your product backlog to ensure you have included technical and functional requirements needed for your release. For example, your first release may require security, infrastructure, organizational and master data objects. Your team should review linkages and handoffs between submodules and modules. This can be achieved by returning to the Story Map, and walking the client again through the end to end processes, to ensure that you have captured all integration points.

There is a logical set of core functionality that must be delivered first. This includes such things as organizational structures and technical infrastructure, amongst others. Following a client's prioritization of the stories, your project team now needs to insert must have SAP technical requirements that are required as predecessors to certain client requirements. These requirements are "enablers" of client process requirements. The team must also make note of the required configuration sequence, and use this to adjust sequencing of the stories. For example, in HCM, certain employee infotypes must be created first. Jobs, positions and organizational units must be defined in the system before the employee can be hired into the organizational structure.

You may also decide, for example, that a transaction level story is too complicated, and you want to break it out to a process variant level, or go even more granular, by selecting a few requirements at that process variant level. For example, in HCM you typically have a number of automated actions as part of the standard PA40 transaction. These might include actions to process new hires, rehires, leave of absences and terminations. A release that attempted to include the full set of hire actions might be too unwieldy for the team. You could consider targeting one of the actions for your first release. You may even decide to select a subset of new hire requirements from the backlog, and focus on one personnel area or employee group.

As part of the slicing exercise it is very useful to schedule a project team workshop to build out a dependency diagram. In this exercise, your team looks again at dependencies between transactions, crossfunctional objects and RICEFW objects. This exercise can drive out further reprioritization of the product backlog (*http://it.toolbox.com/blogs/enterprise-solutions/using-dependency-diagrams-16512*). This whiteboard exercise is an excellent visual tool for ensuring that all dependencies are captured.

A dependency diagram begins with the root structures of the solution – the ones that contain the master data and transactions that everything else builds on. The relationships between the stories are then sketched out. Using a rolling look ahead approach, you can conduct these sessions regularly through the project, as new information comes in.

Traditional waterfall projects are often late because of the cascading effect of late predecessors on their downstream, work packages. It is critical in Agile projects that you perform adequate planning in your releases, to ensure that you build in the right sequence. In this way, you can reduce the effect of late tasks on downstream, work packages. As an Agile developer once told me "if your project has too many dependencies then you are doing something wrong." His comment stems from the Agile goal of creating stories that are completely independent. Although this sounds extreme, it helps emphasize the ultimate goal in development projects, of removing the finish to start risk caused by late tasks impacting their downstream tasks.

Another method of ensuring that you remove the impact of dependencies is suggested by Schwaber and Beedle (*Agile Software Development with Scrum*). Schwaber and Beedle recommend that we partition a large application into several branches anchored by "root objects." The first iteration of realization should develop the minimal set of functionality that "cuts through all the layers of the architecture." For the first sprint, choose backlog items that have both high business value and involve a "root" domain object.

Their concept of root objects is embedded in the fact that most objects build off a logical base of functionality and data. Schwaber and Beedle provide a good SAP applicable example of a payroll system root and branch structure. The root object of an SAP HCM solution is the employee master and its core infotypes. The payroll solution will have nothing to process without the employee master. Further, your solution cannot maintain addresses without the core infotypes, and the benefits module will have nothing to process without the employee. In the benefits module you can identify the various benefits plans as branches in the structure. Employee is the root object. Address, payroll, benefits and benefits plans are branches.

By partitioning SAP into branches, anchored by its root objects, the project can be broken into releases. In a large multiteam project, you would start by building one slice that contains a root object and some branches. Following delivery of this first slice, and its associated infrastructure, you could begin parallel development, by dividing out the various releases amongst the respective project teams.

Each branch has to be decoupled from other branches as much as possible, to reduce dependencies and ensure that each team can work with minimal dependency on the output of another team. So in this example, we would start with a sprint to build the base employee infotypes, and then add in a hiring action, so that other teams could build their own data. We could then split into different project teams, and assign them branches from the various HCM modules.

Figure 7 shows the sample Story Map after it has been divided into releases. Note that stories scheduled for each release are shifted down into their own rows. Grouping the stories in this manner provides a good visual record of the contents of each release.

The client and project have decided to build a first release that includes portions of each HCM module. The first span includes the minimal set of process steps that holds meaning to the client. The critical employee root object is included in the first release, since all other objects build off of this object. In this example only, Release 3 will be released to production. Releases 1 and 2 will be released to the quality assurance system and release activities will include the full cutover exercise.

Depending on the module(s) you are implementing, you will need some organizational and master data objects to be defined during blueprint, since they will be critical to understanding the overall design. In HCM, items, such as the enterprise structure, employee structure, payroll structure, organizational structure and benefit areas, need to be defined in blueprint. Others can be left to realization, and you can create a separate technical story for those objects.

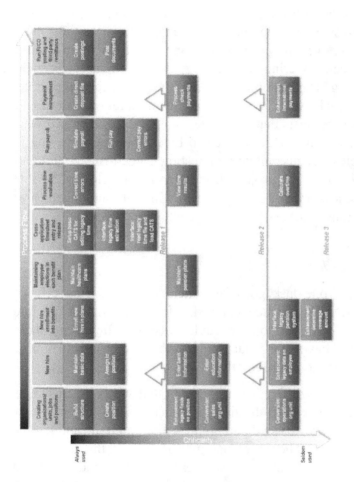

Figure 7: Story Map showing releases

Through building our software in slices of functionality that cross the application, we reduce the need to segregate our test process. In the typical SAP project, we need to plan out functional unit testing, technical unit testing, string testing, integration testing, user acceptance testing, security testing, regression testing, non functional system testing, etc. In Agile, we are performing continual tests throughout the project, covering unit testing, through to user acceptance testing. The customer describes their test acceptance criteria for each story, and as the team solutions stories, the customer tests that the stories integrate together as a whole. There is no longer a need to break integration testing into cycles, because integration testing is occurring continuously throughout the project. It is in the natural flow of SAP that business process steps (stories) will be tested, together with various data sets, to prove the integrated solution.

Dependencies

When one task goes late, there is a cascading effect on downstream, dependent tasks. In waterfall, we are rarely able to recover our schedule once a sufficient number of tasks have gone late. In Agile, we want to manage dependencies differently.

The main difference in Agile is that we build in bite size pieces that are full slices of functionality. These bite size pieces are divided along lines that hold meaning to the customer. The best analogy for this is the tracer bullet analogy. Cohn discusses Hunt and Thomas' recommendation to fire what they call a "tracer bullet," through each story, to ensure that the story includes a piece of each layer of the solution (*Agile Estimating and Planning*). In SAP, our primary layers are database, configuration and development. You want to build in increments that contain a piece of each layer. Let's extend the tracer bullet analogy to planning out the dependencies between our work items.

On a waterfall project we run into issues with dependencies, because we plan our work at the technical task level. A typical realization phase Work Breakdown Structure (WBS) for ASAP, divides the work into the major categories of configuration and development. Within configuration we break it down by modules, and within development we break it down into reports, interfaces, conversions, enhancements, forms and workflow. We take account of dependencies when building the initial schedule. For example, if we know that an interface requires certain configuration, then we schedule a finish to start relationship between those two tasks. If the configuration task goes late, then our interface work cannot start, and the lateness creeps further down the schedule.

The goal of the tracer bullet approach is to plan our project so that pieces of each layer of our application are built as one unit. In our interface example, we would want to schedule the release so that it bundles the interface object together with its related configuration story. For example, if we know we need to build an interface from a legacy timekeeping system, then we would schedule the ABAP for the inbound interface in the same release as the configuration for the CAT2 transaction. Together, these work items would hold meaning to our customer and therefore be releasable. Remember that in Agile we want to always be constructing in such a manner that if at any point we had to stop the project, then what we had built to date would be releasable and usable.

To further the example, a higher level story might read "as a timekeeper, I want to be able to edit hours that have been collected by my legacy time system." In this particular solution, let's suppose that the business process is for hours to be collected through terminals into the legacy timekeeping system, and that editing must take place in SAP following the transfer of those hours through to SAP.

Our larger story then involves extracting time data from the legacy system, reading the file into an SAP ABAP program in real time, and loading the SAP cross application timesheet. We would schedule this story to be completed within the same release. At this point, we need to disaggregate this into smaller, estimable stories, ideally averaging around five days each. Typically, we need a baseline of configuration prior to beginning work on interfaces, so that our interfaces understand the required mappings and translations. We would therefore want to disaggregate into smaller stories, beginning with a piece of configuration that would provide us with a functioning CAT2 transaction. At that point, you have a sufficient base from which to begin work on the interface. In our approach, you want to avoid a story that reads "build the entire interface." Most interfaces require several days to build, and would break our rule of keeping to smaller, work packages. Therefore, a first interface story might read "As a timekeeper, I want to view an employee's name, regular and overtime hours in SAP." The developer assigned to this story would keep to a simple design of coding a mocked up file with one record, and send it to CAT2. Subsequent stories would continue to bite off small pieces of the configuration and development.

Each work item would require team analysis, involving both your time configurator, ABAPPER and the customer.

The configuration and ABAP would be developed for the most part in parallel (the configuration tasks will likely take less time, and your configurator will be able to work on other items, but be available to work with the developer as needed). As stories are completed, the end user would be called to test each story. Subsequent, smaller stories would continue to be built and unit tested until the larger story was complete and ready to be submitted to the "ready for integration testing" queue.

This approach is different from the manner in which we typically approach RICEFW. You will quickly see the advantages and the challenges. The challenge is the increased effort to plan out your RICEFW, so that you better understand the configuration required for each RICEFW. The other challenge is that your configurators must now work more closely with the ABAPPERS, when their preference may be to build their transactions independent of the "gap" requirements, and later return to make any adjustments. But, although this may be a challenge for your configurator, it is, in fact, a significant advantage for your project.

On one project, we had a very complex system landscape, with close to 40 interfaces. I had planned the project using waterfall, and therefore sequenced the project to have the configuration completed first, with interface work beginning once the required configuration had been completed. Unfortunately, on nearly every interface we had significant rework required on the configuration, because we had not understood how intricately linked the business rules were between the interface and the configuration. The interfaces themselves, in fact, drove requirements that the business had been unaware of. This occurred because the larger, legacy system we were replacing, had been in existence for over 20 years. Business users changed, things were not written down, and rules had been coded that most had forgotten.

By using the tracer bullet approach, you help to avoid the risk of discovering new requirements when starting work on the RICEFW. However, you also improve collaboration and speed within your teams. By pairing up the configurator with the ABAPPER, you improve the design of the solution, because both can collaboratively build a better system. Rather than the configurator handing off requirements in a specification, both resources can talk through the design "as it is happening."

The above approach is similar to Poppendiecks' approach for coordinating work between multiple teams. Poppendieck recommends "spanning an application" to build pieces of a solution that "drive a nail through the system" (*Lean Software Development: An Agile Toolkit*). Each piece contains a small amount of functionality from each layer of the application. By using this approach, you can set separate teams to work in parallel on selected spans of the system. For example, one team can work through a span of the benefits module, while another works through a span of the payroll module. Each span would include both configuration and RICEFW. It is not always practical to set more than one team working on a span in the same module, since the same IMG tables would be required by both teams.

Defining "done"

On a traditional SAP project, we define an item as "done" when it has been unit tested. Agile goes much further. As a minimum, an item needs to be string tested before being considered done, but you should seek a standard where items are integration tested as well. This is because we need to be working towards code that is releasable. Even if the project is unable to release to production, we must still have the transports in releasable mode. This means that the related configuration and development must have been integration and acceptance tested (acceptance testing may be done separately from integration testing, if you have an extended business test team that performs a final check). If you can't build integration or acceptance testing into "done," then you will need to schedule stabilization sprints prior to release, where each object is integration and/or acceptance tested.

The work to define "done," must be completed prior to story estimating. This ensures each estimator starts from the same level footing and assumptions. Acceptance testing takes a lot of time in SAP – especially if being done manually. But by baking it into the definition of done, you incrementally bite off pieces of the larger testing effort, rather than saving it all until the end of the project. This means that over time the testing takes less and less time, as the business learns the software and gets more proficient at testing. Adding in a test automation tool to automate regression tests, can make things even faster (test automation is discussed later in the book).

AGILE REGRESSION TESTING

A work item is considered "done" when it has been integration tested. But given that SAP is tightly integrated, we know that future stories will need to be tested together with stories that have already been completed. This means that Agile projects are continually regression testing, to ensure that the new builds do not negatively impact what has already been completed. Your test team will use integration test scripts to continually test new functionality together with old.

Later, I discuss how to build nonfunctionals into your definition of "done." Another item you can build into "done" is the piece of the Business Process Procedure (BPP) that is applicable to the story. In this manner, your BPP training documents can be built gradually and kept to date.

Acceptance tests

Acceptance tests are used in place of detailed requirements specifications (*User Stories Applied: For Agile Software Development*). Like requirements, they give instructions to the developers and configurators on how the work needs to be solutioned. The tests need to be specified by the customer, but with input from the configurator and developer who can also propose tests. Stories will be developed "just enough to pass the test." Tests must be specified "before" coding and configuration begin.

At this point in the project, you only want to gather high level tests to help with sizing the story. Then, immediately prior to working on the story in realization, the tests are revisited, and details are added to build out complete test criteria. The high level tests are also referred to as conditions of satisfaction, since they are conditions that each story must satisfy in order to meet the customer's objectives (Cohn, *Agile Estimating and Planning*).

During blueprint, these high level tests provide "just enough" information to clarify the requirements to the project team, so they can estimate the work. The test identification will be augmented with conversation during blueprint, to help with the estimation. You will know you are adding too many test details if you run out of space in the cell in your worksheet, or on the back of your story card. The purpose here is to leave the details until the point in time when you are ready to work on the story. We are not doing a full, upfront requirements gathering.

You need to start collecting acceptance tests during initial story definition. This process should continue throughout blueprint, to provide the client with sufficient time to think through the desired test criteria. The acceptance tests can initially be noted down on story index cards or sticky notes, and later transferred to the product backlog, where they get tied to their respective story.

As an example, the following acceptance tests might be collected for the story "maintain healthcare plans for employees":

- Two policies for separate employee types
- Four styles within each policy
- Dependent age restrictions.

Another example is the benefits story "able to control enrollment for new hire":

- Able to change benefits for one month following initial hiring
- After one month, the system prevents change of plans for a new hire.

These examples show that you are only looking for an initial, high level of detail. The team should seek "just enough" tests to allow them to estimate the story. You can find more details at *www.scrumalliance.org/articles/414-an-argument-for-comprehensive-user-stories*.

Use all tools at your disposal to collect these acceptance tests. Asking for examples is one method. Whiteboards, process flows, spreadsheets and walkthroughs in SAP, should all be used to help derive acceptance criteria for stories.

Blueprint, high level acceptance tests are not detailed business rules. In the example above, we have simply listed high level criteria that help to define the story. The detailed business rules and logic get collected just prior to the iteration. or just prior to working on the story. Rules can be collected throughout the iteration or project, as part of backlog grooming (backlog grooming is defined in the realization section).

AN ALTERNATIVE VIEW ON ACCEPTANCE TESTS

In pure Agile projects, the acceptance tests are not defined until the sprint or iteration, when the story will be worked on. This is to avoid waste, because the act of defining tests takes time, and can lead to waste if stories are later dropped, or requirements change. However, most clients and consulting firms will find it difficult to exit Blueprint without having defined a comfortable level of requirements. Since the acceptance tests form the major part of the requirements documentation in Agile projects, most clients will prefer to define at least the high level tests in the blueprint phase. But if you are in a very progressive organization, then you should know that it is normal practice in Agile projects to delay test definition until the stories are ready to be worked on.

If it helps the team to think of these as a high level list of "requirements," then that is fine. What is important is that they be testable. This means that once the solution is ready, we should be able to verify the solution by testing against the acceptance tests. Acceptance tests ensure that the configurator understands the objective of the configuration and designs to requirements.

During realization, detailed acceptance tests can be used in place of detailed specifications. For RICEFW objects that are more complex, it is possible that some form of additional specification will be required. For example, interfaces and conversion objects will need to be supplemented with mappings and translations tables. However, in the large majority of configuration and RICEFW, the test cases combined with customer conversations, will be sufficient to guide the design and build process. By avoiding the creation of both requirements specifications and test cases, we reduce the need to keep both documents aligned. This results in less waste than would have been spent in a very, low value document updating activity. In reality, if you have ever written a specification, you have noticed how quickly you were able to convert the requirements statements in test statements. I recall making a first pass at test creation by using the find and replace feature to change "the system shall" statements into "test that" statements, when creating a test case for a specification. There is significant waste in maintaining two documents with much of the same information.

For the configured solution, in addition to test cases that help drive out detailed requirements, an additional document will normally be needed, that records the actual configured IMG values. This is used to ensure knowledge transfer to the sustainment team, and to help tie the configured solution to the stories that drove the settings.

During realization, when you are about to work on the story, you should create separate test cases for each story, and add details to the acceptance tests defined in blueprint. Continue adding details to these tests until you feel that you have adequately clarified the story. At this time, the developers and configurators should focus on adding technical tests, to ensure the story meets any nonfunctional requirements, such as performance, security and error handling. By using a backlog that contains both the story and the acceptance test, you have built in traceability from requirements to test. Each realization test case should be identified by a test ID, so that the ID can be entered into the backlog for the story.

Estimating

In order to complete the release planning exercise, the team needs to estimate the stories, so that it can determine whether the desired set of stories can be completed within the timeframe of the release.

Velocity is an Agile term that refers to the amount of tested functionality the team can deliver in a given period of time. In Scrum, velocity is measured as the sum of story points or ideal days for stories completed within a sprint (story points and ideal days will be discussed shortly). In Kanban, velocity is referred to as "throughput," and it is the number of work items completed within a given timeframe.

It is important to note that Agile does not consider unit testing to define "done" for an item. When Agile talks about delivering working software, it is talking about software that has passed acceptance criteria and is ready to be released to a production environment. This has strong implications in the SAP world. It means that we cannot consider a requirement complete until it has been integration tested. Therefore, our definition of velocity, and our estimates, must factor in time for acceptance testing.

Velocity can be difficult to determine at the beginning of a project. It is best if you can start with a velocity measure from a similar project. If not, then you will need to start with an assumed velocity based on discussion with the team, and adjust once you have actual data. You can adjust the estimates to account for current project risks, such as your team skill level or infrastructure complexities. In addition, you will want to consider the working environment of your client site. If you have client team members that work a maximum of seven and a half hours per day, then you will need to adjust your estimates upwards. On some projects you will find that getting client overtime approved is very difficult, and this can, again, affect your velocity. You'll want to also adjust velocity for expected sickness in the team, vacation and available days per month.

If the client has proposed non SAP, experienced team members from their existing information system department, then you will need to add in a buffer to work, that you anticipate assigning to these client team members. Also consider the number of dependencies amongst your backlog items. Cohn provides a number of excellent suggestions on how to adjust for dependencies, build in buffers, and calculate initial velocities when little feedback has been obtained using the existing project (*Agile Estimating and Planning*).

Once you have calculated velocity, you will obtain story estimates in order to get an approximation of the number of stories that can fit within a given timeframe. It is critical to take note that it is an estimate of work that can be completed – not a guarantee. The velocity provides us with a sufficient enough estimate to plan our releases, and we adjust our plan as the team completes work and adjusts their velocity. You can use velocity to calculate an estimated number of iterations and releases to complete all items in the backlog. This is done by summing the estimates of backlog items for the release, and dividing that by the team velocity for a given time period. This will give you the approximate number of iterations required. For example, if you want to complete 100 story points in the first release, and your 10 team members can complete a total of 30 story points per month, then your first release should be an estimated four months, depending on whether you want to reduce scope, or build in a buffer.

In applying velocity to estimate iterations, the formula does not take into account variations in size between the selected backlog items. For example, you do not need to prepare velocity estimates for items of high complexity, another velocity estimate for medium complexity items, and another for smaller size items. There is good evidence to show that over a large number of work items, the complexity level of work items averages out. Cohn refers to the central limit theorem which tells us that given sufficient samples, the distribution will be approximately normally distributed. This means, although there can be variation between a small set of stories, over the larger set of backlog items, our team's velocity will be able to predict the velocity of future iterations, despite possible variability in individual story sizes (*User Stories Applied for Agile Software Development*).

Another important consideration is that there is a point at which additional effort put into the estimating exercise can become a wasteful activity. There is no way to calculate the exact date of completion. We need to gently remind ourselves, and our clients, that an estimate is an approximation of the size of work effort. It is not the reality.

Traditionally, projects have asked team members to estimate the work effort for technical tasks, by providing the number of days they estimate it will take to complete the task. There are many methods the project manager can then use to evaluate these estimates, such as PERT estimating, where a formula is used to evaluate an optimistic, pessimistic and most likely estimate. The issue with such estimating, as Anderson explains, is the "local safety" that team members build in when being asked to estimate work effort for granular tasks (*Kanban: Successful Evolutionary Change for Your Technology Business*). These buffers add up considerably, and can lead to overestimating the required duration of a project. For this reason, Agile recommends that we estimate at the story level.

There are two main Agile approaches to estimating: story points and ideal time. Story points, as Cohn explains, are units used to indicate the relative size of a story in relation to others. Story points are not meant to indicate time. They are meant to indicate size, complexity and uncertainty. It is up to the team to assess the size of a story, based on information provided by the user. That information should consist primarily of the acceptance tests. Therefore, a key input to estimating is acceptance tests.

WHAT INFORMATION IS NEEDED AS INPUT TO ESTIMATING?

In pure Agile, the team uses conversations with the end user, or product owner, to arrive at the estimates for each story. I recommend that high level acceptance tests be written down for each story, as an input to estimating, for a couple of reasons. SAP projects can be very complex and it is important that the team have enough details and clarity around critical requirements, in order to estimate work appropriately. Also, most vendors and clients expect a minimal set of documentation before being willing to sign off on a blueprint document. I believe that over time a project team will be able to earn the trust required to proceed into realization, with even more reduced documentation. But initially, most teams will need to have at least a minimal set of documentation, and high level acceptance tests will ideally meet that need.

Ideal time is another method for estimating stories. Ideal time represents the time it would take to complete a story if the story was the only thing being worked on, there were no interruptions, and everyone the person needed to complete the work was ready and available. In Scrum, when estimating in ideal time, ideal days are used to estimate the stories, and ideal hours are used to estimate tasks during the sprint.

Story points have the advantage of not being in units of time. Estimates in units of time, such as ideal days, are often taken literally by stakeholders. For example, if the team estimates 10 days of ideal time to complete the CAT2 interface, then the stakeholder will start the clock, and in 10 days of elapsed time, expect the interface to be complete. If the team was unable to complete the interface within the 10 days, then the client will assume that the team is not operating efficiently. However, interruptions do occur, and although it would be ideal for actual time to match ideal time, it can rarely occur in a project environment.

Another issue with ideal time is that as the teams gathers more information on the objects, they may feel they should adjust the ideal time estimate to make it better match the expected effort in time. Whereas, given that story points do not reflect time, just size, and relative size differences between objects typically do not change as much, story points have a longer staying power. For that reason, amongst others, I find that story points are the best choice for estimating. You can find a good list of arguments comparing story points to ideal time in Cohn's *Agile Estimating and Planning.*

The Fibonacci scale is often used when estimating stories. In the Fibonacci scale, each number is the sum of the previous two. A beginning series runs through 0, 1, 2, 3, 5, 8, 13 and 21. A story estimated at eight story points will take four times as long as one estimated at two story points. The difference from ideal days is that we do not know how many days difference. We just know that a story with eight points is relatively four times as big as a story with two points.

The ideal is to try to keep all stories similarly sized, so that you can better estimate and plan the work. Five points is an optimal duration, as it is short enough that the assigned resource can clearly communicate progress towards completion. But definitely, anything higher than 10 will need to be broken down into smaller stories before beginning work on the item. The value of using Fibonacci, is that it reduces the time it takes the team to estimate, because of the gaps in the scale. For example, choosing between five and eight is easier than choosing between seven and eight. By inserting breaks in the scale, you make it easier for your team to arrive at an estimate.

The easiest way to begin estimating, is to ask the team to identify a story that is somewhere in the middle in terms of size and complexity. The team assigns this story a value of five. They then have a starting point, and can use this first story as a comparison measure against the others.

There are a number of useful techniques to aid your team in arriving at their estimates. Planning poker is the most commonly used, and originated with James Grenning (*www.renaissancesoftware.net*). In planning poker, each team member is given a deck of cards where each card has a number from the Fibonacci series. A facilitator selects a story and reads out the acceptance criteria for the story. The product owner will answer any additional clarification questions from the team. Each team member then picks a card, and they all reveal their estimate at the same time. The highest and lowest estimators explain their reasoning to the team. The group discusses, and then continues reestimating, until they all agree on the estimate, or are all close enough that one number can be selected.

Ken Power developed an excellent variation of planning poker that can be used to get estimates more quickly (*www.systemagility.com/?s=silent+grouping*). In silent planning poker (*see Figure 8 on P90*), team members take turns placing stories in columns that have been grouped into the Fibonacci series. To get them started, they should place a medium sized story in the 5 column, for comparison purposes. The team then continues placing cards until all stories are on the board. The next step is done silently, so that the activity runs faster. Team members take turns moving cards around until they are comfortable with the positioning. If a particular story moves around significantly, then it gets added to the parking lot for later discussion. Once all stories stop moving, then call an end to the exercise and hold a discussion to gauge the team's level of comfort with the estimates.

WHAT TO DO WITH EPICS
In the silent planning poker example, the team has assigned four stories in the 13 and 21 point range. These stories are too large for the team to work on. At this point, you have two options. You can ask the team to work with the product owner to break the epics into smaller stories of less than eight points each. Alternatively, you can delay this effort until later in realization, when you are ready to work on the stories.

For distributed teams, the Delphi approach can be used. In this approach, each team member estimates the stories individually. They submit their estimates, and a summarized report is prepared containing the results. Each team member then adjusts their estimate, and this process continues until a sufficient consensus is achieved.

It is also important to note that stories will be difficult to estimate if the team has not had much experience with the functionality needed to solution the story. This can occur quite often with RICEFW objects, such as interfaces. Interfaces can range from very simple to highly complex. You will need to reassure the team that they can give it their best guess, and the estimate will be refined during realization. A "spike" is normally used to investigate stories, such as this. A spike is a short task used to investigate and gain clarity on a complex story. Following the spike, the team will revise the stories' estimate.

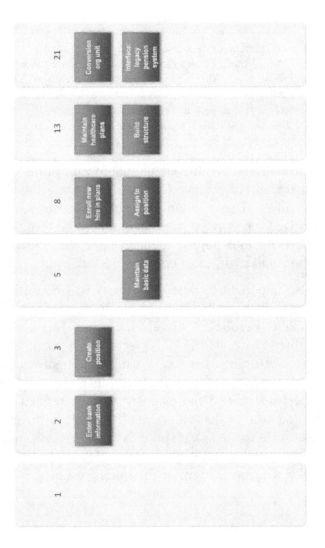

Figure 8: Silent planning poker

A final comment on Story Mapping

There is a less tangible benefit of Story Mapping – customer involvement. On most SAP projects, the customer plays a background role until creation of the business process procedures, and sometimes, even as late as user acceptance testing. In an Agile project, recall that I've mentioned the importance of having full time customers assigned to the project. The Story Mapping exercise is an excellent opportunity to truly involve the customer in designing and taking ownership of the solution.

What is interesting about Story Mapping, is that a tool as simple as sticky notes can yield such significant results. The act of allowing clients to write their own ideas on a sticky note, place them on a board, and move theirs and others around, has a huge benefit. It gets people up out of their chairs, moving around and collaborating! There is an energy to workshops that use sticky notes that still amazes me. This is definitely a tool that you will want to adopt.

On a recent project, I used Story Mapping to identify the client's integration test scenarios and test cases (we left the test steps for a later exercise, given the anticipated number of transactions involved). You can see how this fits into a two tier Story Map of scenario and test cases. On a typical project, we will build out the tests in a spreadsheet or word processor. Knowing about Story Mapping, and knowing that by this late point in the project my team needed a fun and energizing exercise, I decided to apply the concept to test planning.

I assigned the business team some prework of brainstorming test scenarios, and they came up with a list of approximately 300. Many of these were test cases, rather than integrated scenarios, and we would use the Story Mapping exercise to group these into applicable test scenarios.

I was surprised to find resistance to this exercise, not on the part of the client, but on the part of my project team. They worried that the number of test scenarios would be too large to manage with sticky notes (an estimated 200 test scenarios once we grouped the test cases). But in the end, it was the client that pushed for the Story Mapping exercise. In fact, the client lead felt that the downside of having to manage so many sticky notes was far outweighed by the benefit of giving each business team member an opportunity to get hands on in identifying tests. In fact, after describing the exercise to the client project lead, I returned the next day to find that she had purchased several hundred sticky notes, large size post-its and sharpies. The exercise was a significant success, and in one day the business team, together with the consultants, grouped the tests into approximately 200 test scenarios, and documented their associated test cases. The following day was used to prioritize the tests, remove duplicates, and identify test data for each test case.

Nonfunctional requirements

There are a couple of ways to manage nonfunctional requirements, such as performance, hardware and security. Nonfunctionals that are not story specific, such as system performance requirements, can be logged as separate items in the backlog, similar to the way RICEFW are logged. However, most of your nonfunctional requirements should be baked into your definition of done at the story level. For each story, you need to determine the critical nonfunctional tests that must be passed prior to considering that story completed.

NONFUNCTIONALS AND RESOURCE PLANNING
There are resources, such as security experts, who are not typically allocated full time to a project. Their work cannot be baked into the definition of done. You will need to create separate work items in the backlog that can be planned and allocated to them when they are available.

Project documents

Most projects have documents that are not directly related to the user stories. These can include the development approach, interface approach and test approach. In order to track this work, you will need to create work items in the backlog. However, the project must seriously consider whether such documents are value added. There are a high number of potential documents that could be written, but if they are not directly adding value to the customer, then they should be considered waste.

Lean blueprinting

Throughout iteration 0, the project team and customer should be documenting the lean blueprint. The lean blueprint document will be used to record conversations that take place in relation to each process step. The customer must be involved in this effort, in order to ensure ownership of the solution. Having the customer involved will also greatly reduce the review and approval process. The teams should be split into pairs, or smaller groups, containing SAP experts and customer resources. They should write the documents together using a "paired documentation" approach.

The lean blueprint is a process based, solution design. It contains the high level design of how standard SAP transactions can meet the business needs, and how and where development is required to enhance the standard. In other words, it contains your fit/gap information ("fit/gap" is SAP's terminology for identifying the gaps in the solution that will require nonstandard solutions). Unlike the traditional blueprint document, the lean version should not go into detailed design. An Agile project delays details until the moment in realization when work begins on the story related to that activity.

The lean blueprint consists primarily of two documents: the blueprint and the RICEFW list. The blueprint is documented at the process level, with each process being a separate worksheet in a spreadsheet. SAP customers can obtain lean blueprint templates from SAP's ASAP 7.2 methodology. For each process, document the process steps as rows in the spreadsheet. The lean blueprint stops at the process step level. Stories get documented elsewhere in the Story Map and product backlog. The primary columns you will want to be concerned with are: transaction ID, configuration considerations, gap (a yes/no checkbox), RICEFW type (only applicable if a gap is identified), and RICEFW description. You will quickly note that in a spreadsheet it is impossible to enter too much documentation for the configuration considerations and RICEFW object descriptions. This is helpful, since the objective in Agile is to delay decisions until the last possible moment.

PROCESS STEP	ROLE	TRANSACTION	CONFIGURATION CONSIDERATIONS	GAP (Y/N)	RICEFW ID	DESCRIPTION

Figure 9: Lean blueprint layout showing key fields

STORY ID	NAME	DESCRIPTION	COMPLEXITY	LEGACY SYSTEM	DIRECTION	DATA ELEMENTS

Figure 10: Lean RICEFW list showing the interface section

The RICEFW list takes the place of functional specifications in blueprint (detailed requirements for each object will later be built as test cases during realization). The log contains one row per RICEFW, and should provide for different data capture depending on the RICEFW type. For example, selection criteria are specific to reports, and legacy systems are specific to interfaces and conversions. You can identify columns for each object you feel is critical in scoping the related work. Figure 10 provides a sample layout for an interface data collection. As you can see, this is very lean, and a spreadsheet format helps ensure that a limit is placed on the quantity of data captured.

According to the Theory of Constraints (TOC), "inventory" in software development takes the format of requirements (*Agile Management for Software Engineering: Applying the Theory of Constraints for Business Results*). TOC argues the longer it takes to solution requirements, the more risk your project has that requirements will become obsolete. That is, they can go stale due to market changes, or the customer changing their mind. In SAP, we know that the time from when a requirement is originally gathered from the customer in blueprint, to when we actually build and test the solution, can be measured in terms of weeks and months. We know that this is what leads to multiple change requests, and we also know how costly change requests can be in terms of slowing down the project and impacting the go live date. There are other issues with stale requirements. The analyst who gathered all of the details may have left the project, or simply forgotten the details. This leads to rework, when the client needs to explain once again exactly what it is they meant. This type of rework is referred to as "waste" in Agile circles, and our main goal is to reduce waste, because it is costly and detracts from the goals of delivering working software.

In *Lean Software Development: An Agile Toolkit*, Mary and Tom Poppendieck explain that sequential development, in which requirements are established long before development or configuration begins, needlessly imposes high costs on the project when errors are found later during the build process. When the team is forced into making detailed, design decisions long before they will actually build the product, they are prone to many errors. These errors later prove costly, because the client was expected to have "signed off" on these design decisions, and because backing out from a decision can be difficult depending on the amount of predecessor configuration and development that has already been completed. The following quote from their book is pertinent: "Lean software development delays freezing all design decisions as long as possible, because it is easier to change a decision that hasn't been made."

The final reason for delaying these detailed design decisions, is that our objective is to deliver working software as soon as possible. If we spend too much time in documentation mode, then we are not achieving our objective of showing the client working software, so that we can obtain feedback that is critical in ensuring we are building the right product. TOC argues that we are also avoiding the build of costly and useless inventory. Blueprint documents are rarely, if ever, read once the project goes live.

For these reasons, it is critical that the lean blueprint template restricts the analyst's tendency towards verbosity, through the simple mechanism of a limit to the number of characters one can reasonably enter into a spreadsheet cell.

The team should not take too long on the lean blueprint during iteration 0. It is acceptable to allocate half of iteration 0 to documentation. By timeboxing this effort, you indicate to your team the level of documentation expected.

An additional workshop in iteration 0 is required to identify the master data and organizational objects. There is no Agile difference to identifying the master data and organizational objects.

At this point, the project may be ready to proceed to realization. I have included an optional iteration 1 for complex projects, where the client and project team feel they need additional clarification on requirements before committing to realization.

Iteration 1 – First build

Iteration 1 is an option to build in a system validation of the customer requirements gathered in iteration 0. If your earlier solution demo was an external system, then it is quite feasible to return to this system and walk the client again through the processes that you have scoped in the Story Map. However, to get more value from this iteration, build a customer specific system in the client's development environment that can continue to be leveraged during realization. This should not be a sandbox environment, unless you are building a very generic preconfigured system that you do not feel you can leverage going forward. The optimal goal is to use this baseline system as the system for further configuration and development during realization. This avoids throw away work that would have been done in a sandbox environment. SAP best practices provide valuable accelerators when

building   a   solution   demo
(*http://help.sap.com/bestpractices*).   RDS   (Rapid
Deployment Solutions) are preconfigured solutions you can
purchase   from   SAP   to   kick   start   your   projects
(*www.sap.com/solutions/rapid-deployment/index.epx*). With
the right expertise, you can also build these systems
yourself, using downloaded configuration packages, or start
from scratch. Jan Musil of SAP discusses the use of
accelerators to launch your baseline build and subsequent
solution demos to validate requirements:

- **IP reuse**: Use of SAP best practices and
  preconfigured   solutions   to   build   an   SAP
  environment at the client site. SAP allows licensed
  customers to download these preconfigured options,
  and import them into a client system. The best
  practice documents provide process step overviews
  and training documentation, to accompany the
  preconfigured settings. These options are definitely
  worth investigating, since there are a number of
  accelerators. As an example, I have used these to
  help kick start client business process procedures
  (BPP), by providing clients with standard SAP
  BPPs. I've also used them to import sample SAP
  queries into a solution. It is important to note that
  installing an entire baseline solution using these
  preconfigured solutions, is a larger effort, and does
  require experienced configurators.
- **Solution demo approach**: SAP recommends that
  during blueprint the customer be shown a system
  that reflects at least some of their requirements. The
  build of this system can be accelerated using SAP's
  preconfigured solutions, however, there are not
  many configurators who have experience with IP

reuse. If your company lacks experience with IP reuse, you can spend a day or two selecting a subset of the process steps from the Story Map, and an accompanying subset of product backlog requirements, and spend this iteration building a baseline, configured solution. You will want to review the section on release planning for tips on how to slice an SAP project, before beginning the build of your baseline system (*http://scn.sap.com/community/asap-methodology/blog/2010/07/07/implementation-acceleration-techniques--beyond-Agile-methods*).

Note that the baseline system build during blueprint is minimal in functionality. The blueprint baseline in iteration 1 is similar to prototypes you may have learned about in other Agile approaches. This baseline must have a minimal set of functionality. The axiom here is "just enough": just enough functionality that the client can get enough of an understanding of SAP for them to validate their requirements. High risk areas, where the requirements are unclear or complex, should be dissected, so that small pieces are configured to provide the client with a visual they can use to clarify these areas.

Schedule a one or two day solution demo of your system near the end of this iteration. Use the Story Map as a point of reference, by highlighting the processes and process steps that are in scope for your demo. Set expectations by explaining that this demo will include a subset of the client's requirements, and that they should not expect to see the full end to end system. Nor will they be able to walk through every variance of a transaction.

Use the demo to walk through the standard SAP process. In other words, walk through the sunny day scenarios. Explain that the purpose of this demo is not to provide detailed SAP training, but rather, to provide the client with a frame of reference from which to validate their blueprint requirements.

The product owner should be responsible for documenting and capturing any additional requirements that arise during this exercise. At the same time, the Story Map should be updated to capture any additional process steps, including RICEFW. Be sure to ask again about legacy systems at this point, so that you capture all interface requirements.

You should use this workshop to draw out additional information, such as process triggers, expected outputs, and roles and responsibilities. Often the client will leave definition of roles until late in a project, at which time there is a last minute struggle for the security team to define and build the security profiles. It is useful during realization to build test users from the start. This avoids the use of assigning "SAP ALL" during testing, and reduces the time it takes to test and design the security. It can also be useful in helping the client understand, and prepare, their change impact analysis. Use this workshop to help accelerate the client's thinking towards the end state of their working environment. But be sensitive to the fact that the project sponsor may not be ready to reveal the end state in its entirety. Recall that most SAP projects have an efficiency target that often results in new role definitions.

An obvious benefit of acquiring an SAP solution, is to leverage the standard, best practice processes out of the box. At the executive level, they are often quite interested in this approach of using "vanilla SAP," in order to justify the costs of the SAP implementation. However, as you have likely experienced, at the mid management to ground level, you will often find that the client has many arguments for why the SAP standard solution will not meet their requirements. You should strive to include at least some executive level sponsors to your solution demo, so that you gain their support in challenging your audience to think "out of the box" on how they might adapt their as-is processes to the standard SAP solution. In other words, your objective is to discover whether each backlog requirement is truly a requirement, or simply a method to return to their old way of doing things.

CHAPTER 5: REALIZATION

Overview

Before getting into the build phase, it is important to revisit the issue of requirements. In an Agile project, the team has not gathered detailed requirements during blueprint. They have kept things "lean" and focused on ensuring they have captured all stories, but they have not gathered all details pertinent to each story.

As an example, suppose the project is building the benefits module. During blueprint, the team captured the stories concerning savings plans, but did not go into the eligibility rules for savings plans, other than to capture a child story to solution eligibility rules. This is very different from what we have done in the past on SAP projects. The blueprints of waterfall contained pages and pages of detailed instructions and rules.

There are many project teams that get a sense of satisfaction and comfort from capturing and detailing everything in blueprint. There was comfort in feeling that all details are known, and the final part is simply to put hands to keyboard and configure the solution.

The problem is that we all know that is a false comfort. It is nearly impossible for any project team to capture "all" details in a blueprint process document, and this always results in the team arriving at a critical juncture, behind schedule and realizing that requirements were missed. This is followed with the discussion as to whether these are really change requests, or whether the project team failed to capture these in the blueprint document.

An Agile project is about building in a tolerance to change. An Agile project does not therefore attempt to capture every detail during blueprint, because it recognizes that such a task is unrealistic. Business requirements change and project teams miss requirements.

Therefore, at this point, you have your high level requirements in your backlog, but you do not have the details. So, the first step when working on any story, is for your project team to meet with the client to get those detailed requirements.

If an unanticipated story is captured during realization, that can throw the project schedule, then the product owner has more options. Is the requirement valuable enough that it must be added to the project? If yes, are there lower priority requirements that can be removed to accommodate it? If not, then a cost benefit analysis can be performed to determine whether extending the schedule and budget is warranted. By continually delivering working software, the client is able to better judge the value of the remaining requirements.

Testing

Defining tests

At this point you have your Story Map and product backlog. You have a release plan, so you know your delivery targets. Regardless of whether you select Scrum or Kanban for realization, you will need your customer to detail out the acceptance tests for each backlog item. Definition of detailed acceptance tests should be the first activity performed when working on any story. These are your detailed requirements. They tell your team what the target is for each story and how they will get to "done."

It is critical that a definition of "done" for each story includes passing acceptance tests. If we leave acceptance tests, or what we commonly refer to as integration and user acceptance tests, until the very end of the project, then we find that we are back in a waterfall situation. The typical SAP project configures and develops for months before completing integration testing. Often a project will be pressed to meet a fixed go live date and reduce the number of test scripts. This negatively impacts product quality.

An Agile project ensures that acceptance tests are defined "in advance of the build," for each requirement in the backlog. One thing we learn from lean methodologies (*Lean Software Development: An Agile Toolkit*) is that we must delay decisions until the last possible moment. If we do not delay, for example, we gather all detailed acceptance tests during blueprint, then we risk what lean calls "waste." We risk creating waste because requirements change, and with them, the definition of acceptance criteria changes.

So, we do not want the client and team to spend significant time during blueprint to gather detailed, acceptance tests for all requirements. But we do want them to spend time gathering detailed, acceptance tests when first working on a story. This process needs to be explained to the customer during realization kick off. You should provide guidelines to the customer, and let them know your expectations when it comes to acceptance testing.

This method is very different from what we are used to on SAP projects. We normally gather requirements in blueprint, then configure and develop, and finally, gather test scripts. In an Agile project, we must do the reverse. We must ensure that we have the tests gathered "before" we start the build process. There are a number of reasons for working in this manner, but the primary one is that passing tests is the end goal of any build. Therefore, it only makes logical sense to have the test criteria "before" we start the build. This provides the configurators and developers with advance notice of how they need to build the system, so that they can pass the test.

In Agile, we want our teams to do the least amount of work possible to pass the test. This sounds like a rejection of quality, but it is not. The client has defined the tests, and we would be wasting resources if we built more than the client needed. In Agile, we do not build in bells and whistles in order to impress the client. We also do not try to anticipate future needs and build the product so that those future needs will be met. As an example, on one project the team was building an interface from a legacy system into SAP. They knew that in phase two of the project, an additional legacy system would come in scope that would likely leverage the same interface. Their impulse was to design and build the interface today to accommodate the needs of the future legacy system. I had to remind the team that we could not anticipate the exact needs of this legacy system, that things could change any manner of ways between today and the future phase, and that our mandate was to get to go live for our current scope only.

As your customer defines acceptance tests at the story level, they can begin to think about how to string these tests together into integration tests. The identification of integration test scripts is easier in an Agile project because of the use of stories. Given that stories are already in business language, it is easier for your end users to understand how they might string together a group of stories to create a business test scenario. Conversely, in a traditional project, the requirements have been written in a technical language that end users find difficult to understand and interpret. On many projects we have to help the business come up with integration test scenarios, by supplying them with sample test scenarios from other projects. A further benefit of Agile projects is that the end users only need to define integration test scenarios for the set of stories that will be delivered in the next cycle. This gives them plenty of time throughout the project to hone their skills and understanding of how to define test scenarios.

A method of identifying tests that is getting more popular in the Agile world is "Example-Driven development." Crispin and Gregory discuss Example-Driven development in their book, *Agile Testing: A Practical Guide for Testers and Agile Teams*. Example-Driven development suggests that for the more complex stories, we ask the customer to provide us with an example of how they see the solution to that story. This is one manner of defining acceptance tests. For example, if you are building an online CRM web store for purchasing books, you might have a requirement that customers are able to load an online shopping cart with selected books. For that requirement in your backlog, the customer may walk you through an example where a customer opens the CRM online store, selects a specific book, adds the book to the cart, saves, and then opens the cart to check that the book is in the cart.

MANY WAYS TO SAY THE SAME THING

You may also hear the term "Specification by Example" (*http://en.wikipedia.org/wiki/Specification_by_example*). No matter what we call it, examples can be used to further clarify the stories. The examples can complement the acceptance test, or even replace them. You can ask customers to provide realistic examples to clarify requirements to the team. Typically, these examples are framed as: "Do this, then that, then verify this."

Example-driven development is a great method to define and structure tests, because it is intuitive for the customer. The customer can relate to an actual sequence of events that might take place within the application. Often, we struggle to explain what we mean when we ask for a series of test cases and test scripts. By repositioning it in terms of an example, we help translate our needs for a test script into something that the customer can understand.

Defining the test team

Throughout realization, there will be constant testing of the solution. This team needs to be staffed by business resources. On a traditional project, we may not involve business resources in testing until the latter part of integration testing and user acceptance testing. In Agile, our goal is to have continued business involvement in the project.

In the early stages of realization, the business testers will require more of the team's time, in order to learn transactions and the testing process. It can be expected that this will negatively impact initial team velocity and throughput. This will be an explainable impact on speed, as we need to ramp up business knowledge. You will need to continually work to make the business as independent as possible, so that the team can focus their efforts on the build process.

As soon as possible, resources from the sustainment team should also be added to the test team. If the plan is for key project resources to roll onto sustainment, then you will need to take this into account when planning your releases. This will impact your ability to release to production, and may require you to perform the majority, if not all, releases to the quality environment only.

When to test

The goal is to avoid holding separate integration tests iterations (also called "Stabilization Sprints"). The point of Agile is to test often, and always be testing. In Scrum approaches you must run acceptance tests throughout the iteration. In Kanban, you must run acceptance tests once sufficient work items have been unit tested and moved to the "ready for acceptance testing" queue (*see Kanban section*). If, however, your project is highly complex, with numerous interdependencies, then you may need to add an integration testing cycle prior to each release. Holding an integration test cycle prior to release does not mean you stop ongoing acceptance testing. As soon as items are completed in both Scrum and Kanban, you need to have a business team begin acceptance testing of those items.

All of this means a continual testing effort throughout your project. By involving your business users earlier in testing, you catch errors earlier, and ensure the business is trained and ready to run the solution at go live. In Agile, your client will be involved in testing from the very production of working code and configuration. This affects the time it takes to complete stories, since team members will be responding to defects while working on other stories. That is why it is critical that your team understand that the definition of "done" includes the completion of acceptance testing. The estimates of each story and RICEFW object need to take acceptance testing into account.

As each build expands on the previous, your client test team will need to run regression tests, to ensure that the current build does not break anything that was previously passed. To minimize the effort of regression testing, you will want to consider test automation tools. There are SAP test automation tools that allow you to record SAP transactions, and automate the run of tests for those transactions with data you define. It is definitely worth investigating such tools, particularly for large scale projects that will have significant ongoing test efforts.

It is also important to develop nonfunctional tests for items, such as system performance testing, interface connectivity testing, workflow e-mail testing and printer testing. These tests should be planned and built in to the iteration testing, to reduce technical risk at cutover.

RICEFW unit testing

Unit testing is rolled into the development step in Agile methods. The two go hand in hand. The ABAPPER will code a little, test a little, and repeat until both code and test is complete. There is the concept of technical unit tests versus functional unit tests. Traditionally, the ABAPPER only conducts technical unit tests. In Agile, we speed up the process and improve efficiencies by having the ABAPPERs perform both technical and functional tests.

So, you can see there are a number of concepts we need to address here. First is to return to the definition of roles. Many Agile methods prefer to have developers who are both technical and functional. When your developer can speak directly to the user, you greatly accelerate your development process. When your developer is senior enough that they can understand the transactional side of SAP, you can go even further with improving your development process. The objective of a good Agile project should be to engage developers who have business knowledge, SAP transactional knowledge and development technical knowledge. If they don't have the knowledge, then we invest project time upfront in training.

Such a developer is able to perform both the technical and functional unit test steps. However, even if you cannot find such a skilled developer, you should be encouraging your functional tests to be written in such a manner that your developer can run them with a little transactional training. That is another Agile objective – always be training. Investing in team training pays off in the long run. I could argue that it would delay my project if I train my ABAPPERS on how to run the transactions required to functionally test code. However, this falls prey to short term thinking. On a long term project, it is far more valuable to invest time upfront on development team transactional training, in order to save long hours in development and test.

If your developers are able to run their own transactions, then you reduce the pull on your configurators and business people. This increases your capacity on the configuration work stream. If your developers can run their own tests, then the feedback loop between code and requirements is dramatically reduced. If they can run their own tests, then you are reducing waste – and removal of waste is a lean approach to getting "done" faster. Waste in this case would be the time it takes the developer to contact the configurator, get clarification on the requirements, wait for the configurator to run the test, and communicate back the results. Avoiding that waste pays off more than you might think – such waste adds up over the course of a long project. Remember, that your goal as an Agile leader is to maximize the productive time of your team.

AUTOMATED RICEFW TESTING?

Agile methodologies use a number of automated methods to test code. In SAP, we have traditionally used CATTs (Computer Aided Test Tool), eCATT (Extended CATT) and third party tools, to automate transactional testing. However, the practice of applying third party tools to automate testing of SAP RICEFW objects is not widespread. I have therefore not focused on automated RICEFW testing methods. It is useful to be aware of them, in the event they do catch on more in the SAP world. Crispin and Gregory describe that in Test Driven Development (TDD) "the programmer writes a test for a tiny bit of functionality, sees it fail, writes the code that makes it pass, and then moves on to the next tiny bit of functionality" (*Agile Testing: A Practical Guide for Testers and Agile Teams*). If you are looking for pioneers of SAP TDD, Daniel Vocke has written a brief article on how to apply TDD to ABAP using Blue Ruby (*http://scn.sap.com/docs/DOC-10310 – you will need an SDN User ID to access the article*).

So again, it is more efficient, and less waste is created, when the requirements for a RICEFW object are written as test cases. Each story will have had high level acceptance tests identified for it during blueprint. As noted at the beginning of this chapter, the team should delay writing detailed tests until the last possible moment. The team should start writing detailed tests for a story when the story is first worked on. The developer will meet with the configurator, or user (depending on who best understands the requirement), to discuss and clarify the tests prior to beginning development.

Configuration unit testing

As in traditional projects, most configuration unit testing will need to be done manually, given that most tests are continually being updated to reflect the latest configuration change. However, there is value to reviewing transactional tests to determine where it might make sense to automate. This is especially useful when building regression tests that can be run against each new release.

Third party testing tools can provide you with the capability of recording transactions, and loading variables to auto run those transactions. SAP eCATT is a cost effective, though less robust, tool, to automate transactional testing.

The drawback about automated SAP transactional testing is that it is not simple to set up. It requires significant knowledge to set up and maintain the tool. However, the rewards can be significant. By automating your testing, you can save significant time.

A final note on testing

On an SAP project, we often build in silos. We have configuration teams, interface teams, conversion teams, training teams and business teams. As much as possible, you should avoid these silos. There is a very compelling reason why Scrum avoids titles when referring to team members. Everyone is a "developer," because that way there is more reason for them to help each other and collaborate.

One of the biggest failures of our waterfall approaches has been to build these silos into our teams. By their very nature, Agile approaches provide us with better opportunities to build in collaboration in place of competition. In Scrum, everyone is a developer, and the "team" works together to reach the iteration goal. In Kanban, everyone meets daily to review the work and "swarm" any bottlenecks, by providing each other with the help they need in order to overcome the issues they are each encountering ("swarming" is often referred to by David Anderson when addressing the action of the team members to collaboratively address a given problem).

Agile testing, then, is about helping each other reach the end target of passing acceptance tests. It is not about finding problems with what another team built. It is not about pointing fingers at how one team did not focus on quality, or looked for short cuts. It is about finding bugs, and helping each other resolve those bugs as efficiently and effectively as possible.

Backlog grooming

Backlog grooming is a Scrum approach, but can, and should, be applied to both Kanban and Scrum. Sutherland, in his *Scrum Handbook*, suggests that five to 10 percent of each Sprint should be dedicated to clarifying requirements, splitting large stories into smaller and estimating items. A regularly scheduled weekly meeting can be used, or this activity can be managed ad hoc. During this activity, the product owner should also revisit the prioritization of work items. By keeping the backlog "groomed," the project ensures that a constant stream of backlog items is ready to be worked on.

Scrum

When to use Scrum

Ultimately, I've provided you with two sound methods to running Agile SAP projects. Both Kanban and Scrum will work well when you marry them to your organization's and project's particular needs. My guidelines on the choice between Scrum and Kanban are here to help you make that choice.

Scrum deemphasizes experts. If your project is highly dependent on a few key experts, then Scrum may not work well for you. The reason for this is because of the many dependencies on a large SAP project. A Scrum Team of five to nine people must be productive "as a team." If the majority of members are waiting for two others to complete a large set of tasks, then the velocity of the team will be negatively affected. That said, if your project can absorb training and knowledge transfer, then you may be able to leverage Scrum to transfer some expert knowledge to the remainder of your team. Future sprints would then flow more smoothly.

Scrum will also be more difficult if your project team is distributed geographically. Earlier, I mentioned some techniques for managing a distributed, Scrum Team, however, it is certain that a Scrum Team is more effective when colocated.

SAP sprints

Overview

Previously, you broke your project into releases. You now need to break those releases into iterations. In Scrum, these iterations can be of two weeks or one month, or some other variation, depending on the scope of your project and the amount of time it will take your team to build something of value to the client. Given the complexity of most SAP projects, it is likely best to begin with one month sprints, and adjust later if need be.

An iteration is a full cycle that includes planning, analysis, design, coding and configuration, unit testing and acceptance testing. You will see below how each works within a sprint.

Sprint planning

Each sprint needs to kick off with a one day workshop. Attendees must include the users, product owner and Scrum Team. The output of sprint planning is the sprint backlog. The sprint backlog is a subset of the product backlog. It contains only the backlog items that will be attempted during the sprint. It also contains tasks required to complete each backlog item. That is the main difference between a sprint backlog and a product backlog. The sprint backlog contains the tasks for each story, estimated in ideal hours, required to complete each requirement.

5: Realization

STORY	TASK	ESTIMATE	DAILY ESTIMATES OF WORK REMAINING		
			1	2	3
Interface: Outbound legacy pension system					
	Analyze legacy system	10	5		
	Write SAP test case	6	4		
	Write legacy test case	5	7		
	Prepare test scripts and test data	8	8		
	Code SAP extractor	11	11		
	Code legacy import	14	14		
	Test	12	12		
	Fix ABAP defects	6	6		
	Fix legacy defects	6	6		

Auto enroll employee in pension following two years			
Analyze requirements	10	6	
Build test case	5	3	

Figure 11: Sample sprint backlog

The sample sprint backlog shows two stories, and the tasks the team identified for each story. The remainder of the worksheet contains the initial estimate, followed by columns for each day in the sprint. The team estimates the remaining hours on a daily basis for each task. The sum of this column can be used to chart a sprint burndown (discussed later).

The first half of the workshop is for the group to review the product backlog, and identify the stories that will be worked on during the sprint. An input to this is the release plan. The release plan identified the high level goals for the release. Now the team needs to select stories that will help them meet the release goal.

The product backlog has already been sorted according to priority, so the team should find it easy to review and select the high priority items relevant to the sprint. The difficult part now comes as the team must select using two criteria: items it has time to deliver, and items that will allow them to deliver a cohesive system.

The goal of an iteration is to deliver working software. In Agile terms, they refer to this as "potentially shippable software." Scrum sprints are designed so that at any time the product owner can stop the team and tell them to initiate cutover, to put their working solution into the production system. This means that the selected backlog items must be capable of working together to create a workable system.

If the team does not feel capable to complete the relevant backlog, based on past throughput or their own ideas about their capacity, then they need to discuss with the product owner what items can be removed from the sprint. Alternatively, the team can discuss which items can be modified to create a simpler design or fewer capabilities. In other words, a given requirement can often be solutioned more than one way. At one end of the spectrum you have a manual solution which is solved through a business process. At the other, you have a fully automated solution which may require a development enhancement. The team can discuss with the product owner whether a middle ground, or even the manual solution, is acceptable for this iteration.

The second half of the sprint planning meeting is for the team to clarify the selected backlog items, in order to come up with an initial design and build approach. The team dissects each story and identifies the tasks required to solution each story. For example, a story to build a standing purchase order type may have an "analysis" task for the configurator to meet with the client to get detailed design requirements applicable to the standing order. Another task for the standing order would then include several configuration activities. This would be followed by a unit testing activity and acceptance testing activity. RICEFW objects include tasks for analysis, design, development and testing.

Each task in Scrum is recommended to be no longer than 16 hours, and no smaller than four hours. This serves as the estimate of work for the task, and the sum of these estimates is the total estimated work for the sprint. Tasks are kept small enough to ensure that the team is able to complete something every day. Also, keeping them small ensures that the task is manageable enough to be feasible for the team to complete it. It moves the team towards progress and completion of deliverables. Smaller tasks move more quickly through a system, and reduce the number of bottlenecks. Smaller tasks also ensure that a team member better understands the complexity of an item, and can therefore turn to others more quickly for help.

The estimate for each task should be in "ideal hours." Ideal hours are hours where the team must assume that they will only be working on that task. They will not be interrupted, and all prerequisites are completed so that the team member can begin immediately.

ESTIMATING IN HOURS IS MUDA

In Lean circles, the Japanese term "Muda" is often used in place of the term "Waste." Hours estimating can take up a lot of the team's time and energy. Rather than use hours estimates, you can have a rule of thumb that each task is one day. Alternatively, avoid estimating tasks altogether – just count them. You can do a sprint burndown, showing a count of tasks remaining, with the assurance that over time the duration of each task will pretty much average out to one day.

Throughout the sprint, the team can add and remove tasks as required. This initial brainstorming of tasks is to provide the team with action items, so that they can hit the sprint running. It is expected that the team will be unable to identify all tasks upfront. There are some stories that will require some analysis before tasks can be identified. Scrum refers to these prerequisite analysis tasks as "spikes." Once the spike is completed, the team can break out the tasks needed to complete the item.

Tracking the work

The work gets tracked at two levels: the sprint level and the release level. Sprint level tracking involves monitoring at the task level. Release tracking monitors at the story level.

In the release burndown, the team gets credit for a story when the story has been completed during the sprint. A story is only considered complete when it has been tested and is ready for release. Partially completed stories are not credited. This serves two purposes: it helps the team learn to improve their scheduling and ensure that they get the work done within the sprint; and it provides a meaningful report to the customer because it tracks at the story level. This is the difference in the audience for a sprint versus a release burndown. The sprint burndown is really designed for the team, because it tells the team the estimated amount of tasks remaining for the sprint. A customer will not understand the technical tasks, so cannot get an impression of how much value has really been delivered during a sprint. A release burndown will give the customer a sense of the amount of value delivered, and the amount of value yet to be delivered.

The release burndown in Figure 12 shows that the project has targeted 150 story points for the first release, consisting of three iterations. In the first sprint, the team was unable to complete the targeted number of story points. In the second sprint, you can see that the team is starting to get back on track. At this point in the release, the team will need to discuss with the product owner whether the final sprint target should be reduced.

The sprint burndown in Figure 13 shows a sprint target of 250 ideal hours. Three days into the sprint, the team realized it had underestimated the complexity of work and had to increase the remaining work effort. This brought the estimated work above the desired trend line. The team then worked to catch up, and is trending back towards the desired rate.

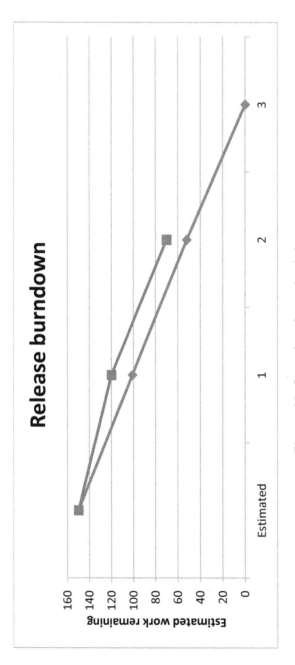

Figure 12: Sample release burndown

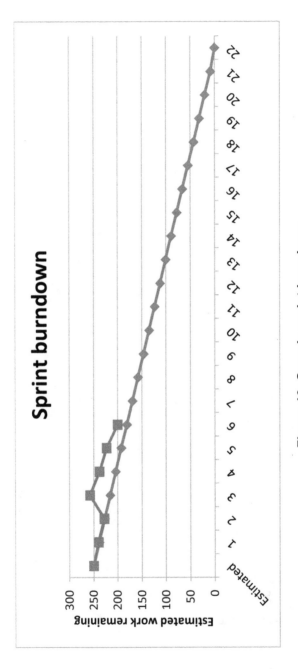

Figure 13: Sample sprint burndown

The ScrumMaster should begin the sprint by building the sprint burndown chart. The burndown chart is used to determine whether the team will complete the tasks within the sprint. It is a line graph that maps total remaining work against the number of days in the sprint.

Each day the team must update the remaining work for each task. If a task was initially estimated to be 16 hours, then following the first day of work on that item, the team member might reduce the remaining work to 10 hours. The next day the team member may meet with the client and discover that the item is more complex than expected. At this point, they might choose to partition the task into three tasks, for example, each with a remaining work of 10 days. At the end of this day, the burndown chart will show a spike to reflect the increase in total remaining hours for the sprint.

The burndown chart is a simple mechanism to track the progress of the sprint. It can be used as a discussion point for communicating what causes spikes in the line, or drops. For example, towards the end of a sprint the team may realize it cannot complete all tasks and barter with the product owner to remove some requirements. The burndown would then show a sharp drop to reflect the drop in total remaining work.

The burndown is a trend line that can be used to estimate whether the team will complete its work in the time allotted to the sprint. The simplest method to measure likelihood of meeting the completion date is to use a ruler to connect the beginning point on the y axis (total estimated work for the sprint) to the final targeted point on the x axis (last day in the sprint). If the burndown line is not trending towards the last day in the sprint, then you may be in trouble of not making it.

As in any project, if the team appears that they are not going to get the work done in the allotted time, you have several actions you can take. However, there are some actions that are unique to Scrum that we will discuss. Normal procedures include resolving issues that are blocking the team. For example, the team could be held up because a required resource external to the team is not available. Another problem may be the team's approach to getting the work done. A review can be held to determine if the team can move forward by using a different approach. For example, on one project the client had guidelines that a developer should conduct a technical specification review prior to coding. The developer was unable to reach the reviewer, who had gone on vacation, so the developer put things on hold and moved on to other noncritical work. A simple policy clarification allowed us to reassure the developer that a specification review was not mandatory for coding to begin.

Other options to improve velocity include reducing scope, or adding resources. Both options are difficult, however, the optimal option here is to reduce scope. Adding resources does not always increase velocity. The team would need to break, in order to provide knowledge transfer, and the new team member may be days to weeks before being productive. Reducing scope can take many forms. Backlog items can simply be removed from the sprint after negotiation with the product owner. Alternately, the solution to a backlog item can be simplified for this sprint, and, if need be, enhanced in a later sprint.

Specific to Scrum, a final solution includes aborting the sprint. In Scrum, a sprint is never extended to accommodate late work items. The sprint is always time boxed so that the team gets better at determining what they can commit to during the sprint, and ensuring that they actually complete the work during the sprint. It should be rare that you have to terminate a sprint, but if things are so bad that the team is unable to deliver any working software, or there are other issues, such as a lack of support from management, then the team and ScrumMaster can consider an early termination of the sprint. This obviously has strong political ramifications, and if not done carefully, it can appear that the project team is not the best fit for the project. This is even more pronounced if the project team is an outside vendor. Therefore, early termination of a sprint is an option that must be considered very carefully.

Daily Scrums

The daily Scrum is a 15 minute daily meeting used to synchronize work between the team. Never refer to the daily Scrum as a "status" meeting, because the objective of the Scrum is not to report status to the ScrumMaster. The objective is to coordinate tasks. The ScrumMaster must avoid becoming viewed as a directive leader of the work. This can be difficult for most developers who are used to reporting to a project manager. Completion of the work is to be owned by the developers. The ScrumMaster is there to facilitate the meeting and remove obstacles.

When I first started running daily Scrums, I found team members would report to me when they were talking. They had understood that the purpose of the daily Scrum was for me to monitor their work and ensure they were getting it done. To avoid this, I revisited the purpose of the daily meeting, and reminded the team that it was really their meeting – not mine. I also found that by not always making eye contact when a person was giving an update, they avoided falling into the habit of "reporting to me." This encouraged them to look at other team members, and they eventually fell into the habit of speaking to each other.

The format of a daily Scrum is simple. Each team member should respond to the following three questions:

- What did you do yesterday?
- What will you do today?
- What's in your way?

It's important to share what was done yesterday and what will be done today, so that other team members know whether they can start a dependent task. They can also provide suggestions on how best to approach the task, or even offer to take one of the tasks. The answers also serve as commitments to each other that they will get a piece of work done within the next few hours.

By talking about what is in their way, they communicate obstacles. These obstacles should be recorded on a whiteboard, and the ScrumMaster must make a commitment to get these resolved in the shortest time possible, because the team is under commitment to deliver the sprint backlog by the end of the sprint. Most decisions should be made on the spot, and the project charter should be structured to empower the team to make decisions.

I have run a daily sprint with some members being remote, by using a teleconference number and a WebEx. Setting up the meeting can take a few minutes, and this work must fall to the ScrumMaster. Again, the ScrumMaster is there to keep the team focused on getting the work done, and lower value tasks, such as running meetings, must fall to the ScrumMaster.

The daily Scrum is not for finding solutions to issues, or determining how to get work done. The ScrumMaster needs to control these discussions and defer them to follow up meetings. Typically, the follow up meetings will occur immediately following the daily Scrum.

In terms of meeting room logistics, your Scrum room should have a door, speakerphone, table and whiteboards.

Getting the work done

A Scrum Team must be protected from outside interference. That is, the team must be allowed to work only on the backlog items identified for the sprint. In a typical project, we schedule all manner of meetings for team members. We constantly shift priorities and reassign new work to team members. These sorts of distracters dramatically slow the speed at which team members can complete work.

In a sprint, the ScrumMaster and product owner have the job of protecting the team members. Any meetings during the sprint must only be related to the work being completed during that sprint, and ideally, it should only be the Scrum Team that schedules these meetings, since they are the ones ultimately held responsible for completing the sprint work.

The work for the sprint is defined in the sprint backlog. No other work should be allowed to take place during the sprint. This point is critical. We cannot shift priorities during a sprint and, realistically, things should not change that dramatically within a 30 day sprint that we cannot wait until the next sprint to insert any new work. We cannot deflect the team from their sprint backlog, because at the end of the sprint, the team will be judged on their effectiveness to plan and complete work during a sprint.

In learning about Agile projects, you may wonder when the detailed analysis and requirements gathering takes place. As mentioned earlier, Poppendieck argues that we should delay decisions until as late as possible. On our waterfall SAP projects, we did an upfront gathering of all requirements and configuration considerations. Then, later in realization, we often found that things had changed, or we had missed details. This frequently resulted in the client having to reiterate their requirements to the team. On an Agile project, we delay this detailed analysis until the team is ready to work on the requirement.

As the team starts working on the backlog items, they meet with the client to work through the finer details of the solution. This analysis task then allows both the client and developer, or configurator, to agree on the finer requirements and intricacies of the design. The information is fresh in both of their minds, and their next step is to define the acceptance test for the backlog item. Both analysis and definition of test occur *before* configuration and development take place. The team member now has the latest requirements information, plus the target, in the form of test criteria needed to ensure that the development and configuration are completed in the most effective manner.

During the sprint, the team needs to ensure that their documentation is kept up to date. This includes updating configuration design documentation, test cases, specifications, and any other required deliverables. This is critical, because the goal of Scrum is to provide the customer with the opportunity to stop the project at any time and release to production.

In waterfall SAP, we leave training documentation, typically called Business Process Procedures (BPPs), until the final stages of realization. In Scrum, we need to ensure that user documentation is built alongside each sprint. Ideally, the customer test team will contain members responsible for training documentation. Through testing, the training team will learn the business process, and gain the knowledge necessary to prepare the documentation.

Another standard SAP deliverable is the configuration design document. Most clients expect this as a formal deliverable when handing off to sustainment. If the team is accountable for these documents, then the project should determine whether these will be documented during the sprint, or as part of the release effort. The argument for delaying this until release, is to avoid rework in updating the document, each sprint, for the same IMG activities.

Each sprint must include the full set of tests: functional unit testing, technical unit testing, string testing, integration testing, user acceptance testing, security testing, regression testing, nonfunctional system testing, etc. This must be taken into consideration during sprint planning, to ensure sufficient time and business resources. As sprints progress, the regression testing effort will intensify. Automated testing tools can help reduce this impact, but if not available, then the team should strive to simplify the testing process, by using test templates that are not labor intensive to prepare and complete.

Defects should be fixed immediately, and resolution of defects should be baked into the definition of done for each story. However, it is likely that defects will escape into future, sprint regression testing. These defects must be prioritized, and if found to be high priority, added to the top of the product backlog, so that they are worked on as close as possible to when the team actually solutioned the story.

Sprint review and retrospective

At the end of the sprint, the team holds a one day session that is split into a review and a retrospective. The review meeting is to identify which stories were fully completed, and then demo this working solution to various stakeholders. The points for each completed story are added up to calculate the velocity of the team. This velocity will be used to help project the number of stories that the team will be able to complete during the next sprint.

The sprint demo must be kept to a half day, and should be of an informal format. This is because, in Scrum, the time spent formatting presentations is considered low value. The sprint demo is the client's opportunity to see what was produced during the sprint.

The sprint retrospective is used to improve the process. The team is asked what went well and what can be improved. This process will feel strange to a traditional project manager, who is not used to involving the team in decision making. But that is one of Scrum's strengths. Decision making and processes are improved by having team members involved. They are more likely to take ownership of a process improvement when they were involved in its design. The optimal goal of these retrospectives is to improve team velocity.

Kanban

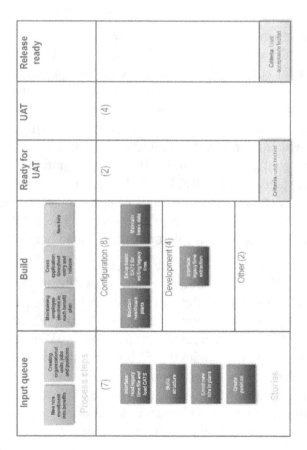

Figure 14: Sample Kanban board

Building the board

On large, SAP waterfall projects, we typically track the configuration and RICEFW work through project plans and status reports. Kanban provides us with a much more visual method of tracking and communicating progress.

A Kanban board example is shown in Figure 14. A board is typically divided into vertical and horizontal sections. The vertical columns represent steps in your process. A typical SAP configuration approach in the realization phase, involves the following sequential steps: detailed analysis and design of what was blueprinted, configuration of related Implementation Guide (IMG) activities, unit test of the configuration, and finally, integration and user acceptance testing. RICEFW objects follow a similar flow, from detailed analysis and design, to code, unit test, integration and user acceptance testing. These steps can be mapped into vertical columns on a Kanban board.

Horizontal swim lanes are sometimes used on a board to map different work item types. These swim lanes can be used to highlight differences between work items, based on priority or work item size. For example, defects are typically assigned a higher priority, and you can ensure that their priority is quickly visible, by showing them in a different swim lane. Another option for tracking high priority items, as opposed to swim lanes, is to flag the work item card visually. Different colored cards can be used, for example, to highlight different work item types.

There is one significant difference to the sequential steps in a Kanban board versus a traditional project process. Traditional SAP realization phases conduct unit testing at the object level, and leave integration testing until all objects in scope have been unit tested. This results in a huge backlog of items waiting to be integration tested. As with Scrum, Kanban ensures that the project is continually integration testing and user acceptance testing. Therefore, your board must have a final column called "user acceptance testing."

Given that acceptance testing applies to more than one story, you will need to complete a minimal number of stories prior to beginning user acceptance testing. For this reason, you'll need a queue on your board called "test ready." Once stories have been unit tested, you can move them to the "test ready" column, to signify to the test team that they can begin integration testing as soon as they have a sufficient number of stories in the queue.

Integration testing and user acceptance testing will often be the same on an Agile project, since you will have the business users continually performing the integration tests. If, however, you want to bring on additional business testers to perform user acceptance testing, then you'll need separate columns for integration and user acceptance testing, respectively.

Value stream mapping can be an excellent method of identifying the steps in your process, because it provides a method to identify steps that do not value (*Lean Software Development: An Agile Toolkit*). In value stream mapping, you follow work items through your process. You need to follow a good sampling of items, including configuration, development, security, etc. Chart out the value stream as a process flow, and identify, for each step, the amount of time that a work item sits in that step. You also want to record how much time a work item waits in a queue for the next step to begin. For example, if at a certain point in your process, work items sit idle waiting for someone to sign off, then you need to record that as a "waiting activity." This process forces you to step back and critically analyze each step, to see if it truly adds value. It also gives you the initial leadtime to process a work item, and your objective through Kanban will be to reduce this leadtime.

Your goal should be to keep the design of the board as simple as possible, so that it is easier to step back and get a visual of the entire project. If your project is large enough, it may make sense to build separate boards for each team. Unlike in Scrum, where a team size of seven plus or minus two is prescribed, there is no set team size in Kanban. You will need to use your judgment. In his book, Anderson relates how one project used a Kanban board to manage the work of over 50 people. In my own experience, I've managed a team of 20 with one board.

What is evident is that smaller teams are easier to manage. There is a strong argument in Agile that you should keep your team sizes small. Typical standards are anywhere between five and 10. However, the smaller the teams on a large SAP project, the more Kanban boards you will need to manage and coordinate.

What Kanban teaches us though, is that we should experiment and continue to refine our process. Kanban recognizes the complexities of projects, and does not expect us to "get it right the first time." As you learn more about Kanban, you'll learn how various projects have gone through several layouts of their Kanban board. Each layout is the result of process improvements that the team underwent. You need to experiment on your project to determine the optimal team size and layout for your board. Ensure that your project team receives training on Kanban.

The team needs to understand the importance of continually improving your process.

The most important component of both Scrum and Kanban is that the project works as a collaborative team. Traditionally, we have separated teams on an SAP project by module and development. In Kanban, by having all work show on the same board, we are better able to show the team how each of their work items impacts others. This allows us to begin a project with a collaborative approach.

In fact, Anderson uses an interesting word for describing how a team reacts to road blocks that prevent work from getting done. A team should "swarm" blocks to resolve them collaboratively. On more traditional projects, we often find that each team member focuses more directly on their own work. If another team member is held up, it is generally accepted that they, or the project manager, are individually responsible for resolving the issue. In Kanban, we turn this around, and instead encourage the team to help each other. Collaborative behavior gets encouraged by the project manager during the daily meeting, with the question "what can we do to help?" Kanban encourages us to succeed as a team.

Stages in a Kanban board can have buffers, to identify work that is ready to be moved to the next section. These buffers are typically used to manage bottlenecks at a specific step in the process. Bottlenecks are discussed later, but essentially, these are steps in your flow where work takes a long time to be processed. Inserting a buffer column prior to the bottleneck, helps ensure that the bottleneck always has work to keep them busy. Given that work takes a long time to be processed by the bottleneck, it is important that time is never lost by having the bottleneck sit idle. The buffer size should be the smallest size possible required to ensure that the bottleneck resource is never idle. The buffer will ensure that work items are always ready to be worked on by the bottleneck.

A Kanban board should always begin on the left with an input queue. This queue can also be named "to do." It is the input queue that directs the ongoing work. The project manager and business owners should move work into the input queue from the product backlog. With the backlog carefully sorted by priority and release plan, the input queue is continually getting refreshed with the work items that should be completed next.

Anderson suggests that the input queue should contain enough work to keep the team busy for one week. You do not want to overload the input queue, because the team will get distracted. Our human tendency is to want to tackle all open work items at once. By limiting the number of work items that appear in the input queue, you reduce distractions for the team, and keep them focused on the work at hand.

Your product backlog will contain both the higher level stories (at the process step level), and the lower level stories. Your product backlog needs to link the parents to the children, and identify the planned release for the children. Earlier, I discussed a layout of the backlog that contained a column for the parent, a column for the children, and a column for the release. In this manner you can quickly filter at the parent level, and identify all relevant children and their associated release.

Anderson suggests a method for you to track both levels of work items in your Kanban board. You can place a swim lane at the top of your Kanban board to contain the process steps. The lower level stories can be tracked in a swim lane below. Child stories can be linked to their parents by placing the parent's ID number on the child's work item. The main value of tracking both children and parent is for you to communicate more clearly to your customer the work that is in process. The customer will be more familiar with the higher level work items from the Story Map.

There is another method to communicate the items being worked on. As soon as a child item is pulled onto the Kanban board, you can flag the related parent on the Story Map. In this manner, your client will be made aware of the stories being worked on.

If the higher level stories are not planned to be completed in the current release, you will need to clearly communicate the portion of work planned for completion in the current release. In this, I mean that you will often need to break a higher level story into multiple releases, and you'll need a method to communicate which piece is active in the current release. This can be as simple as making a note on the parent card on the Story Map, as to which piece is currently being implemented. For example, a purchase order transaction story on the Story Map may be partitioned into multiple releases. The first release might build the standard purchase order type. The second might focus on standing orders, and a third might focus on service orders.

As mentioned, you should be prepared for your Kanban board layout to change over time. This will naturally occur as you optimize your development process. The layout is not the most important thing about Kanban. What is most important is the focus on creating a pull system, and learning to optimize development processes.

For simplicity, the Kanban board in Figure 14 assumes there are 10 team members, consisting of four configurators (one personnel administration/organizational management, one benefits, one time and one pay), two developers, one security expert and three testers. A WIP limit of two per person is assumed (WIP limits are discussed in the next section), giving a total WIP limit of "in process" work of 20. This example assumes that this team's average throughput per week is five, and the input queue WIP limit has been bumped up to seven, to account for variations between weeks. The build stage includes both the analysis and design for each work item. Process steps (parent stories) are tracked in the upper swim lane, as their related child stories get pulled into the input queue. The "ready for UAT" buffer column is used to moderate the flow of items hitting the small test team. This buffer allows the non testers to complete an additional two items above the test WIP limit of six, thereby allowing them to increase their production. If the "ready for UAT" and "UAT" columns WIP limits are reached, then the non testers will be advised to take on testing responsibilities, in order to move items off the board.

WHY COMBINE ANALYSIS AND DESIGN WITH BUILD?

You will often see a separate column for analysis and design, because in many projects these activities are distinct in themselves. I have presented only one of many possible board layouts. Often when a team member is configuring something, they will cycle between analysis, design and configuration, until the object is complete. For that reason, I have combined those three activities in one column. My example also assumes that the developer is performing both analysis and code. This is not always the case, and if in your project you partition the analysis and code activities between different team members, then you will need separate columns.

BOARD WIP LIMIT VERSUS COLUMN WIP LIMITS

In my example, the team's WIP limit is 20, however, the board shows a total limit of 27. I tend towards having the team's WIP limit apply only to items in a build stage. This allows me to ensure that each team member has at least two items to work on at all times. This ensures that each team member can pull in a second item if one becomes blocked. But it is up to you how to manage your WIP limits. The important thing is to experiment with WIP limits until you achieve a desirable flow and output.

Configuration on an SAP project normally follows a similar flow to development. In both cases, analysis will be performed on the work item, to build out the test case and determine the best design. The steps of build and test are similar for both. There can be some differences in the build phase for development. Particularly for interfaces where a work item may need to go through both a legacy team analysis and code, and an SAP team analysis and code. If that is the case, then you can add additional steps within the build phase to allow for the legacy and SAP work. What is different between configuration and development is the team composition. Configurators typically perform their own analysis and build, whereas developers do not always perform analysis (although it is worth considering, since it will reduce your leadtime by having developers perform analysis). In development, you may have analysts working along with developers. If that is the case, then you need to add vertical sections to manage the separate WIP limits for analysts and developers.

For configuration, you may feel a need to add swim lanes for each module. This might be useful if you have a large team divided by module, and you want to have a better visual of the work moving through each module. However, be careful that you do not end up with a board that is too complex to manage. Simple is best. The fewer sections you have on your board, the easier it will be to review and manage the work during each daily meeting. As an alternative to adding sections by module, you could use a story naming convention that identifies the module.

Kanban boards can be built on a physical wall using sticky notes, or cards pinned to a cork board. A physical board is an excellent rallying point for daily meetings. There is much to be said for the collaboration and team involvement that takes place when everyone can get hands on to adjust work on the board. However, in today's SAP projects, where work is completed by distributed teams, you'll need to invest time in an electronic version of the Kanban board.

The simplest way to create an electronic Kanban board is to use a spreadsheet. There are also online Kanban tools that are much more robust, and have a professional appearance that a spreadsheet cannot achieve. It can be worth your time investigating the online tools.

Some examples of online Kanban tools include:

- Agilezen
- *www.Trello.com*
- Jira greenhopper
- *www.Targetprocess.com*
- Cardmapping
- *www.kanbantool.com*.

Work in progress

The first time you build a Kanban board, and place your deliverables onto the board, you will likely be surprised to see how much work is currently "in process." This section discusses the value of placing limits on the amount of work in progress. If you have ever had issues on a project where too many deliverables were at 90% for too long a period, then you have already experienced the pitfalls of allowing the team to start too many concurrent activities.

You will have noticed that both Kanban and Scrum use visual boards to manage the work (Scrum does not prescribe the use of a board, however, most Scrum Teams use a board to visually track the work, and to gather around for their daily Scrums). There is one distinct difference between a Kanban board and a Scrum board. This difference explains why Kanban is unique and effective. Kanban boards have Work in Progress (WIP) limits. Anderson found that by applying WIP limits to the activities of the team, you can increase throughput and reduce leadtimes (*Kanban: Successful Evolutionary Change for Your Technology Business*).

Remember when constructing your board that you need to ensure a WIP limit is respected for each resource. Setting a WIP limit requires you to consider the team's capacity. But this is simpler than you might think. Kanban recognizes that multitasking does not work. Therefore, a rule of thumb is to assume that each team member can work on a maximum of two items at one time. By having two items, if one item gets blocked, the person can continue working on the other item. You normally do not want to set a limit greater than two per person, because you want to keep items moving, and avoid teams getting bogged down with multitasking. But do not set the WIP limit yourself. You need to discuss with each team member to ensure you get buy in. Some team members may insist on having a WIP limit higher than two. If so, start with their requested limit, and adjust downwards if you find that work is building up at their station.

You need to be careful not to place too strict a WIP limit on work at the beginning. Tight WIP limits of one per person are difficult to manage on a project with a lot of dependencies. An SAP project, with all of its complexities, will normally have many dependencies. Given the likelihood that some work items will be waiting for prerequisite items to complete, it is important to provide a resource with an option to switch to a different task.

Your WIP limit applies to both the items in progress and the items that are sitting in a buffer (a queue holding done items in a given stage). For example, the configuration step may have a buffer for items ready for acceptance testing. The WIP limit for configuration must include configuration items that are still being worked on, plus the items that are ready for acceptance testing. This is an important concept. If you apply your WIP limit to only the configuration items in progress, then the "ready for acceptance testing" buffer will have an unlimited WIP limit. The number of these items will eventually overwhelm the testers' capacity to test them. You would effectively be creating a bottleneck at the testing stage, as items stop flowing at that step.

Having a WIP limit apply to buffer, can result in a step having no items in progress – they will all be in a done state. This is completely acceptable, and results in what is called "slack" time. Slack time is important. Traditionally, project managers are tasked to keep all resources at full capacity. It seems that as soon as a resource is idle, the sponsor starts thinking about cost reduction. This is a wrong assumption. By rolling off idle resources, you will end up costing the project more money, not less (this assumes that the idle resource is not idle for an over extended period of time).

Resources on an Agile project should be expected to see periods of slack time. On one project, I had a developer idle for two weeks. The PMO started to question whether we should roll off the developer. I had to explain that the project was currently moving at the speed of an upstream bottleneck. Once we got work through that bottleneck, the work would again hit the developer. In the meantime, the developer spent time optimizing existing code. It is the nature of projects that work will get bottlenecked. Kanban provides a number of methods to address bottlenecks. But the key is that you never want to schedule resources at full capacity, because slack time is not only inevitable – it is needed.

Having slack can be useful when the team hits a wall and needs additional support. In the case of my bottleneck example, the developer did not have the knowledge to help relieve the bottleneck. Instead, the developer worked on optimizing code. In XP, this activity is called refactoring. Refactoring is the process where developers revisit existing code to simplify design and reduce development times (_www.xprogramming.com/book/whatisxp/_). By having slack time, the team can engage in process improvement activities that otherwise would not be performed.

On an SAP project, you will need to watch activities assigned to your specialists on the Kanban board. The expertise of a module configurator is often needed in many places on the project. At any one time, a configurator might be configuring, mapping conversions, providing design input to a RICEFW object, and helping a business person test a transaction. It is easy to assign work to a specialist.

There is always a need for them. What is harder is saying "no" and respecting your WIP limits. I often found it was not the configurator who broke the WIP limit – it was me as the project manager. This sets a dangerous precedent. If you, as the lead, do not respect the policies of your Kanban board, then you cannot expect your team members to do so.

By breaking the WIP limits, you set yourself up to create bottlenecks. Before long, your specialist has far more work than they are able to close, and all downstream steps get blocked, as they wait for prerequisite tasks to complete. It is true that for consultants there is almost an expectation that consultants should take on larger WIP limits, that they should work late into the evening to complete outstanding work, and often this plays itself out in reality.

Some team members can work 10 hour days for weeks. I'm sure we all know people who work 10 hour days, six days a week, for months. I'm sure we are all familiar with these "superstars." The trouble is that even they can burn themselves out. If a project is so understaffed that resources need to work continual overtime, then the project runs the risk of losing resources, and one cannot assume that everyone can equally perform to this level. We cannot plan in overtime for an excessive duration to meet a deadline.

Ironically, by setting WIP limits we improve the team performance. By keeping multitasking to a strict minimum, we reduce the time it takes a person to complete a task. WIP limits therefore reduce the need for overtime, in order to meet a date. If the project reaches a point where overtime would be required for an extended period in order to meet a date, then a discussion can take place with the project sponsor.

Prolonged overtime may fool all of us into thinking we are getting more done with less, but it eventually catches up with us. Team members either get exhausted, and future performance suffers, or we find out that the team member has many work items "in progress," but none finished. Getting those items to a state of "done" becomes harder and harder, because the resource is continually switching gears, mentally, between the multitude of open tasks.

You may wonder whether Scrum limits work in progress. In fact it does, through the design of its sprints. Only a certain number of product backlog items are allowed into a sprint. However, Scrum, unfortunately, does not prevent a resource from starting multiple tasks at once, and keeping them all open until the end of the sprint. A ScrumMaster, then, needs to be aware of the danger of having too much in progress, and communicate this to the team at each daily Scrum.

The daily standup

The daily standup is similar to a daily Scrum, but it does not ask team members what they worked on yesterday, or what they plan on working on today. The Kanban board, itself, answers those questions for us. The focus in a Kanban daily is on the blocks, maintaining flow and coordinating the work.

Unlike a Scrum daily, a Kanban daily can involve more than nine participants. By not needing to hold a round table, the Kanban daily reduces the number of actively contributing participants in the meeting. A daily meeting should start by discussing any items that are blocked. In my spreadsheet Kanban board, I highlight blocked items with a stop sign and high priority items with an exclamation mark. I begin the meeting by asking the owner of each high priority work item whether they are on track to resolve the issue. I use that opportunity to gauge whether I, as project manager, need to help resolve the issue, or whether I need to ask the broader team for help.

Once I've gone through the high priority items, I move to discussing items that have not moved for some time. As soon as a work item is pulled from the input queue, I have the team mark the start date of the work item. In the daily, I am then able to quickly identify items that have been open for some time. Oftentimes, you will discover "hidden work items" during this part of the meeting. If an item has not moved, the assigned team member often relates that they have been spending time on something else. You then need to add that other work item to the board, if the WIP limit allows, and use this opportunity to remind the entire team of the Kanban policy – all work must be tracked on the Kanban board. Team members must be instructed not to work on anything that is not on the Kanban board. This is how you manage priorities and ensure that the project is working on items that the product owner identified as priority. The team member may convince you that the other item is important, but it is not yours, or their decision, as to its level of importance, in relation to all of the remaining work on the board and in the product backlog.

I have often found that team members will be pulled into work that non project leadership believes is critical. This other work may be business as usual activities, but it may also be work that someone deemed critical to the project. The issue is that the work was not identified in the product backlog. On one project, I discovered that client team members were pulled aside for two days to assess a number of reports, to determine their level of complexity, and arrive at an assessment of work effort. As the project manager, I was not informed of this task, and only discovered it at the daily meeting when I asked why a work item had not moved since the previous week. The team members felt they needed to perform the sizing effort, because it was their organizational manager who asked them to perform it.

The daily meeting is your opportunity to keep the team focused on delivering the priority work in the desired timeframe. The team quickly gets used to 15 minutes being sufficient time to complete this important task.

The input queue

The input queue is the first column on the Kanban board. It needs to get replenished from your product backlog. Alternatively, if your project scope is small enough, then you may not require a product backlog, and you can replenish directly from your Story Map. In that case, I would suggest you pull stories directly from your Story Map into your Kanban input queue, and flag the story card on the map as "in process."

You should replenish your input queue on a weekly basis. Anderson suggests that you determine your team's weekly throughput, add a small buffer to that number, and use that as the WIP limit for your input queue. You want to be sure that there is always sufficient work ready for the team to start. However, obviously it's good news if your team moves ahead of schedule and pulls all items from the input queue prior to you replenishing it. To replenish, you simply pull in the next priority items from the backlog until the queue is full, or you have removed all items applicable to the current release. Once you complete work items for release, then you are ready to run a final preparation phase.

Pulling versus pushing work

A core Kanban principle is that of allowing the team members to pull work. Traditionally, the project manager pushes work onto team members according to project demand. This often results in over allocation of work, and the subsequent issues of having too much work in progress. Kanban instructs us to allow team members to signal when they are ready for more work. The WIP limits act as these signals. This ensures that work is getting pulled according to the team's capacity, rather than according to some external demand.

Once a WIP limit is reached, the team member does not have any more capacity to accept new work. But if the number of work items falls below the WIP limit, the team member is ready to pull in additional work. Essentially a free slot has opened, and the next priority work item can be moved into the slot.

What work types do we track?

The Kanban board must show all deliverables that hold value to the customer. I put an emphasis on the word "deliverables." The Kanban board should not track tasks that hold no meaning to the customer. It is here where Kanban diverges from Scrum. Scrum sprints track tasks for each story. When the team reports on performance in a sprint, they are reporting on performance as it relates to technical tasks. Often these tasks are too technical to hold meaning for the customer.

Kanban is about tracking value. There is a lot of evidence behind Kanban to show that a project should only track items that hold value and meaning to a customer. It is simple for you to do this. Only track stories on your Kanban board. Your customer will have written the stories, and will have a good understanding of the value the story is expected to deliver. If the team members feel they need to track tasks for associated items on the board, then they should do so outside of the Kanban board.

Imagine your typical SAP project plan where you are tracking IMG activities, specifications, code and unit testing. Informing the customer that 10 of 40 IMG activities have been completed, does not give them a sense of value for money or time. A separate issue is that it can fool even the project manager into thinking things are better than they are. Your configurators may tell you that the majority of their IMG activities are complete, but until the business has tested the related transactions, you have no idea how ahead or behind you are on your project tasks. Testing may reveal that the configuration was done incorrectly, or that configuration settings were missing. It is for this reason that we only track stories in Kanban.

Work item size

The Kanban board must contain all work that the team is working on, with some minor exceptions. Common sense will tell us that tracking a one hour meeting or a 15 minute task, will not add value. So, work items with a relatively small duration do not need to be tracked, provided they cannot be grouped into one large work item. For example, a single defect may take only one hour to fix, but if your project has a number of those defects, then you can group them as one work item. The ideal length of time for a story to move from "in process" to "done," is three to seven days. Anything longer, and you risk that your team may not have understood the full complexity of the story. You have likely had tasks of a much longer duration on your projects, and will have had to report them as 90% complete for weeks on end. The 90% reporting problem can occur when the assigned team member does not have a true sense of the real work remaining, due to missing and misunderstood requirements.

I encourage you to strive to have all stories be the same size. This will help with planning delivery dates, and it will ensure that work items remain manageable for the team. Large work items can contain hidden complexities, and be difficult to predict completion dates. A target of having all stories be five days duration, or even three days duration, can be defined as a Kanban policy for your project. If, after the first day, a team member finds that a story is in fact larger than the target, the story can quickly be broken down into multiple stories to ensure the target is maintained.

In the Story Map you identified child stories for each parent process step. A process step is often solutioned by a transaction, a variant of transaction or a RICEFW object. A transaction variant might be, for example, the HCM PA40 transaction for actions. An HCM project will have several actions, including, for example, hiring, rehiring, terminations and retirement. These actions are all initiated within the PA40 transaction. Any one of these actions can take longer than a week to configure, unit and integration test. You therefore disaggregated the PA40 action into several child stories. Each child story will be configured and tested separately.

Similarly, most RICEFW objects will take longer than a week to analyze, develop, unit and integration test. On a traditional SAP project, we size and schedule RICEFW objects as a whole. Highly complex RICEFW objects can take up to a month, or longer, to develop and unit test alone – and that is excluding integration testing. Agile is clear on work item size. We have already discussed the pitfalls of large work items, and even traditional PMI principles agree that tasks should be of a manageable size. We need to break down the RICEFW stories into their smaller components.

At first, one might think to divide a RICEFW object along the lines of specification, code and test. The issue with this is that we should always be focusing on work items that have value to the customer. By creating a work item for the specification, we have no software to show the client once that specification reaches done. Also, a specification work item would not follow the flow of our Kanban board. A specification work item would not be coded or tested. And finally, our optimal goal is to code with test documents. We want to minimize the number of detailed requirements specifications, since they can quickly become waste in our process. For these reasons I would not recommend dividing a development work item along the specification, code and test lines.

So we want to look for disaggregation methods that focus on producing functional software. The activity of disaggregation should be conducted as a brainstorming exercise, with relevant team members. But one example might help. Suppose we have a legacy, time management system that tracks all scheduled and actual hours worked for employees. On our project, we need those hours to post into SAP, so that they can be edited and approved in the time management module, and then subsequently run through SAP payroll. A good interface team will naturally focus on attacking an inbound interface of this complexity in steps. At a high level, they would first look at the data objects, to determine if they could segregate along those lines. This could include segregation between salaried and casual employees, for example. They would need to map the legacy data to its SAP equivalents. This would identify any required translations. They would determine whether an ETL (Extract, Transform and Load) tool should be used to perform any translations and file manipulations. Following this, they would want to work on the legacy outbound process, to create a sample extract file. The next major step would be to code the inbound SAP interface and perform an initial import. In this example, you can see several ways to dissect the work for the team. Work items might include:

- Extract and translate salaried data from legacy system
- Extract and translate casual data from legacy system
- Mock up import and call CAT2
- Import salaried data into SAP time module
- Import casual data into SAP time module.

If division along the employee type would not reduce the work effort, then the team could look at other possible means to reduce a work item, until it is roughly five days to analyze, code, unit test and acceptance test.

Finally, you want your team to do concurrent analysis of related configuration and RICEFW objects where it makes sense. This will be important when you suspect that a RICEFW has the potential to introduce configuration requirements. Referring back to our Kanban example, the configuration of CAT2 has the potential to be impacted by

5: Realization

the legacy interface design. You want to put the parent story of "enter time in CATS" in progress, and perform the initial analysis of CAT2 and the legacy interface, concurrently.

A final point here is that if after a day of working on a story, the team still has no idea how long it will take to complete the work item, then you need to split the story immediately. This implies that at your daily standups you are asking teams to validate the backlog estimate for each story on the board. This is a critical point, since often teams will begin work, but not worry about communicating the completion date. Given the multiple reasons for keeping work items at a smaller size, it is important to educate your teams on the importance of communicating, if they think the backlog estimate was dramatically understated, or the SLA is unachievable. Otherwise, your leadtime and throughput targets will get thrown off by a large work item that the team is unable to close out. This has the ripple effect of negatively impacting your release plan target.

Failing that, your team communicates that it is having difficulty with a work item, your fall back in Kanban is to track the start date of work items. For every work item that moves into process, enter the start date. Then use your daily standups to address the slow movers. A developer informed me he had lost faith in Kanban, because he felt that it did not help things move faster. He explained that their board had multiple work items that had not moved in weeks. Unfortunately for them, the issue was not with Kanban, it was with that project's failure to actively apply Kanban principles. A number of problems were apparent in that team's misapplication of Kanban:

- Their work items were too large, so they took too long to move off of the board, and the team therefore lost interest in monitoring the board.
- The project manager was not actively working to remove issues and road blocks that were preventing some work items from moving forward.
- The team was not "swarming" the blocks to remove them.

As I've heard mentioned, Agile is simple, but it's not easy. The principles are simple. It is not difficult to understand the core principles behind Agile techniques like Scrum and Kanban, but it is hard to apply them. Kanban quickly reveals the problems in your process; it's up to you to address them. The good thing is that Kanban provides many tools for you to use to improve your processes and keep things moving.

Using Kanban to improve

Kanban has a close cousin called Kaizen. Kaizen is the Japanese term for continual improvement. It involves incremental improvements and elimination of waste. Waste is anything that adds cost but no value. Anderson discusses a Kaizen culture as one where individuals "spontaneously swarm on problems, discuss options, and implement fixes and improvements." Anderson goes on to discuss that Kanban is similarly meant to introduce gradual improvements to your project and organization. Through transparency achieved by the Kanban board and daily meetings, teams are able to see the effect their efforts can have on helping the project as a whole. The Kanban WIP limits have the effect of "stopping the line," and thereby freeing impacted resources to go and help those who are encountering problems. By using the pull mechanism, resources feel more empowered about their work, take ownership, and are more inclined to want to improve the process to increase throughput and quality. As you can see, the techniques that we have discussed earlier all coalesce to drive the project towards a culture of continuous improvement.

On one of my traditionally managed projects, I had structured the teams along functional lines. I had three main teams divided into configuration, conversion and interfaces. The configuration team was further divided by module. Each team would meet separately to coordinate their respective work items. There were additional specialist areas, such as security, architecture, basis, change management and training. Each of these divisions served to create friction between teams. As tasks went late, the dependent, downstream team would get angry at the upstream team for making them "look bad," as they were unable to start and complete their dependent work. Prior to applying Kanban, I attempted to address this friction by helping the slower team catch up, so that the downstream team could get moving on their work. This helped alleviate some of the concerns, but it did not remove the "us versus them" mentality that had crept into the project.

Once I applied Kanban, it was quite startling to see the transformation. By building the Kanban board, we saw immediately one view of all "in process" work for the project. We could quickly see where the bottlenecks and blocks were located, and where the slow movers were. But best of all, we could do this as a team. I canceled the separate team meetings and replaced them all with a 15 minute daily meeting. Attendees included anyone who had open work items on the board. I now had everyone in the same meeting.

For the first week, I kept the meeting focused on the blocks, and took every effort to resolve issues, so that work could start flowing again. The downstream teams were now able to see that we were actively addressing issues that were impacting their work. At one meeting, I decided to actively ask the downstream team members to help the first team. It's unfortunate, but on this project, we had arrived at a place where team members were not actively seeking to help each other. I had to ask two or three more times to encourage the team to offer suggestions. It was very refreshing to see the number of ideas that started flowing once the team members got actively involved.

Leadtime and throughput

Kanban offers a number of techniques for improving throughput and reducing leadtime. Just as in traditional projects, it is important to monitor performance against targets, such as throughput and leadtime. Figure 15 shows a sample report you can use to monitor throughput targets. You will also want to produce a report showing average leadtime and due date performance. You can find samples of these, and the following reports, in *Kanban: Successful Evolutionary Change for Your Technology Business.* Due date performance reports show work items where you have set a hard, due date because of perhaps a downstream, dependent work item. Leadtime performance is a method of tracking against a target SLA. On average, your work item size should be five to 10 days, so on average, you would want to target perhaps, seven days, to turn around a work item from start to finish.

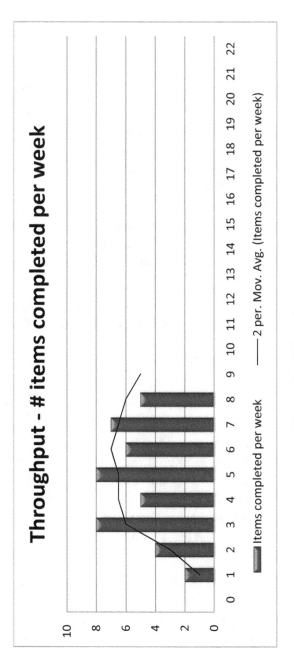

Figure 15: Throughput report

A simple table report comparing targeted leadtime and average leadtime, for a given timeframe, will be sufficient. For due date performance, you can calculate the percentage of actual completion date to due date, and report this in a table format.

To ensure that you focus your team on leadtime, it is important to set leadtime targets. These should become Service Level Agreements (SLAs) that you provide your customer, so that they have a sense of when they can expect a work item to be completed. This also communicates to your team the importance of leadtime. These must be treated as formal agreements with the customer, and you need your team to treat them as serious targets.

When a card moves into process, you should record both the start date and the due date. For items with hard dates, simply record the fixed date. For others, calculate the due date based on the SLA. Once a card is complete, record the completion date. You can then calculate the leadtime, and compare that to your target. If you are using an electronic Kanban tool, then the tool will normally calculate the leadtime.

Similarly, you can help improve leadtime by tracking throughput. I would suggest you track throughput at a weekly interval. Simply add up the number of work items completed each week. You can report this as a trend over time, with the goal of increasing throughput as the project progresses. In Figure 15, the team's objective is seven items completed per week.

Throughput can also be used to indicate approximate completion time, in a similar manner that velocity is used to calculate completion in Scrum. Assuming that your work items are all similarly sized, if your team completes 10 work items per week, and you have a total of 100 items remaining in the backlog, then you can roughly calculate another 10 weeks left on your project. If using throughput to calculate finish dates, you can use this as a checkpoint against your story point estimates. Sum up the story points of the work items completed to calculate a team velocity. The sum of the story points remaining in the backlog can then be divided by the velocity, to calculate an estimated completion date. You now have two completion dates to use as comparison.

There is a huge risk to having work items in an unfinished state for long periods of time. The risk increases as the number of unfinished work increases. The risk lays primarily in timeliness of requirements. Requirements grow stale after a long period of time. Business needs change, and the value drivers of a requirement six months ago, may not be applicable today.

There are other risks to unfinished work. The longer an item remains in an open state, the harder it becomes to close it. Team members forget what their intent was in the design they proposed back in blueprint. The longer an item remains open, the more we risk losing vital design information, and the more expensive it becomes to retrieve that information. Team members change on a project, and loss of a team member who had numerous open items can cause serious project issues. That is why loss of team members on a project is considered one of the highest project risks. This sort of risk is much greater on a waterfall project.

Kanban addresses the risk of stale requirements by delaying detailed analysis, design, construction and test until the latest possible time. By keeping all four components close together in time, the project ensures that it works only on items that hold value "today." The project also reduces the time it takes to fix bugs. Having a team member work on a defect for an item that was configured weeks, or even months ago, requires the team member to invest considerable time to understand the original design intent. Through its application of continual testing, Agile techniques, like Kanban and Scrum, reduce both the number of defects, and the effort required to fix defects, by reducing the duration between design and test. Less rework means better throughput and leadtimes.

Your objective in Kanban is to reduce leadtime. You can reduce leadtime by managing WIP limits carefully. The higher the WIP limit, the longer the leadtime. This occurs because, as you assign more and more work to a team member, they take longer to close any one item. Shifting between work items takes time. In manufacturing, they refer to the time it takes to shift to a different work item as "setup time." In software development, setup time occurs when someone has to mentally shift gears in order to prepare to work on something different.

We want to reduce leadtime for a number of reasons. A shorter leadtime means we are delivering value to the customer more quickly. It also gains customer trust, since they see that the project is able to deliver on a regular basis. Leadtime targets, in the forms of SLAs, provide teams with a target. Teams need targets – in fact they will ask you for due dates – and an SLA is an effective manner for providing these targets to the team. The SLAs are also effective for communicating your project plan at the micro level. The release plan will communicate the stories targeted for a certain date. The SLAs can be used in weekly status reporting, to communicate how well the team is performing against the target dates.

If your leadtime is suffering, it is most likely due to oversized stories, bottlenecks, blocks or waste. Bottlenecks occur when work items pile up at a given resource. Blocks occur when an unresolved issue is stopping someone from completing a work item. Waste is any activity that costs the project in time, money or resources, but does not add value to the customer.

Bottlenecks

Anderson provides a number of methods to optimize a bottleneck. Here are some that I have found particularly applicable to SAP projects:

- Ensure that they are always active. This means that you should ensure they are never in a waiting state, meaning, for example, waiting for requirements clarification, or for another resource to complete a dependent activity. In theory of constraints (*Agile Management for Software Engineering: Applying the Theory of Constraints for Business Results*), Anderson discusses the importance of elevating the constraint – your bottleneck. This means that the project must focus all of its activities on addressing the slowdown at the bottleneck.

- Make sure they are not processing requirements that are incomplete. Incomplete requirements can mean rework, and time lost by a constrained resource in meetings with the user. If you have the option of inserting a different resource to work on the requirements for the bottleneck resource, then you should exploit that option. In Agile, our requirements are in the form of stories. Normally, the story is written high level enough that we anticipate that time will be spent in analysis to get the details. Usually, the person performing the development or configuration is the best person to perform the analysis, however, this is not always possible. If you are finding that your bottleneck resource is spending too much time in analysis, then determine whether a different resource can perform the analysis, and feed the details to the bottleneck to be constructed.

- Ensure that the bottleneck is only working on items approved for work. Your Kanban input queue should ensure that this occurs, however, we know that many team members will venture off onto work that they alone feel is critical. It is important for you to be aware of all in process tasks that the bottleneck is performing. You then need to perform a check against the Kanban board and the backlog, to ensure that the resource has not initiated work that was not identified as critical. It may well be that the resource has identified critical work, but it must be run by the client to get their decision. The team must always pull work from the input queue. All new work must be evaluated by the project manager and business sponsor, to ensure that it is critical in the larger picture.

- Review the existing workload of the bottleneck and determine whether other non bottleneck team members can take some of the work. Quite often, you will have other configurators, for example, who have some knowledge of the modules owned by the bottleneck resource. You may be able to offload some low and medium complexity configuration items to these other team members. In addition, there may be some configuration or development activities that are time consuming, but that do not require significant expertise. For example, configurators most often maintain spreadsheets for IMG activities that require a lot of entries, such as pay scales for a large corporation. The transfer of this data to the IMG can be performed by a non bottleneck resource. Similarly, on the development workstream, the creation of test data for a specific object can be performed by someone given sufficient training on the transactions. Finally, a word about analysis. We often assume that only a functional person can do the analysis for a development object. This is not always true. Keeping in mind the skills of your developers, you need to ask whether there are any situations where the developers could perform the analysis of an object. This would greatly free up a bottleneck at an analysis resource. And again, if you have a separate test team, you can ask whether the developer can do the testing themselves for any objects.

- Finally, your last resort is to onboard another resource and share out the core work to the new resource. This requires you to find an expert with the same skill set, and you need to consider the ramp up time for this new resource.

Blocks

To manage blocks, you need to first visually identify them on the board. Blocks are anything that prevents a work item from proceeding across the board. By visually tagging them, you make them stand out amongst the work items. On a traditional project, we report issues in an issues log, and highlight the critical ones on status reports, but we often fail to have a regular and timely process of reviewing and addressing issues. In Kanban, we record them directly on the board, by first blocking the card of a work item that is held up by an issue. This can be done with a different colored sticky, or an icon on an electronic board. We then have the team work to unblock the card. As Anderson suggests, the entire team should "swarm" the block until it is resolved.

Note that if the block is caused by something external to the project, such as a third party supplier, you may need to create a separate section on your board for "items blocked by external." These items typically require the help of resources outside the scope of your project, and therefore follow a different flow than ones under your control. If the item is anticipated to be blocked for an extended period of time, then you will want to consider temporarily increasing your WIP limit.

In order to continual improve, you will want to record and report on the number of days a work item is held up by issues. This can serve as an additional key performance indicator, to monitor whether your project is getting better at resolving issues. A high number of blocked items can point to underlying problems, and root cause analysis (RCA) can be used to ensure that such an issue does not reoccur. There are many methods for performing RCA, such as Ishikawa diagrams (fishbone diagrams), however, I like the simpler method used by Toyota. Liker's *The Toyota Way: 14 Management Principles from the World's Greatest Manufacturer,* discusses Toyota's "Five Why Analysis" RCA process. The process is as simple as asking why something occurred, then taking the response, and asking why that one occurred. As Liker points out, the root cause is often found upstream in the process.

I can recall one example where the five why analysis would have helped. The interface team was late on a number of critical objects. I assumed that the cause was within the interface team, so I first looked for ways to improve the development process. This provided only a minimal improvement. It took several attempts by the interface team before they could convince me that the problem lay with one of the configuration teams. Had I begun with the five why process, I would have moved much more quickly to the correct cause, and saved considerable time on the project.

Waste

Waste is any activity that does not add value to the customer. Large information systems have developed processes, procedures and documents over the years that, at one time, were perceived to have value. A major challenge of an Agile SAP project is to convince the IS department that some of the activities are wasteful, and not adding value to your project. In fact, beyond not adding value, these activities cost time and money to your client.

When building an aggressive schedule, you need to do all that you can to keep the team focused on activities that are value adding. This is not an easy task, and can require some politically sensitive work to restructure and improve IT processes within the organization. It is best to approach any change as "temporary" and an "exception." In other words, seek to get an exception for your project. A "let's try it out and see" attitude, can be easier to digest for any organization, than attempting a formal process change. It will be important to level set everyone in the project charter that your project is based on a number of assumptions, including the need to bring its own methodology and approach in order to meet its forecasted targets.

As project managers, we are often in the difficult situation of having to meet the IS department's needs for documentation, and balance that with the business desire to reduce project costs and improve the schedule. Review the following, and ask whether your project has been guilty of performing any of these activities. Poppendieck and Poppendieck (*Lean Software Development: An Agile Toolkit*) have identified these seven wastes of software development:

- **Partially done work**: Partially done work is work that cannot be valued. It may be stated as 90% done, but the remaining 10% can be difficult to estimate. Partially done work suffers the longer it is kept in this state, because requirements grow stale. It also leads to the perception that the project is unable to complete work. Projects need to earn the client's trust, and trust is not earned when you continually report that you have a high number of activities in progress but few done.
- **Extra processes**: Customer sign off, change request management and traceability processes, are the

worst offender in this category. The main issue is documentation that does not lead to code. On SAP projects we can spend weeks getting sign off on a blueprint. This occurs because our blueprint documents are so complex that the client does not understand them, but also because our traditional projects warn customers that if it is not in the blueprint document, then it will not get done. In Agile, we accept that changes will occur and details will not appear until we get into realization.

- **Extra features**: I mentioned earlier the story of an analyst who asked the developer to build in some extra features, because she knew that in one year a legacy system would be decommissioned that could leverage the added functionality. This is a major source of waste. We cannot predict what will be needed in a year's time. But most of all, the client is paying for functionality that they need today – they should not be expected to pay for something that "may" be needed sometime in the future.

- **Task switching**: Multitasking is a major source of waste. Kanban WIP limits will ensure you do not fall back into task switching.

- **Waiting**: A lean approach helps ensure that a work item moves through the development process with minimal delays. This is achieved through smaller work packages that flow across the value stream more quickly.

- **Motion**: This speaks to how your project area is laid out. You want to achieve an open, work space with colocation, so that your team members do not waste time walking to get answers. This also speaks to document handoffs. You want to minimize the number of stages through which a document must flow. On one project, I remember we had an elaborate approval process for work items. Prior to starting work on something, the task owner had to describe a work package in a three page document. This was a document about a document. We then had to submit this document to get it approved by the team leads of the areas impacted. Once approved, we could begin work. The intention was good – in the past this vendor had obviously had issues with teams working on non value added work, or else approaching the work ineffectively. However, by holding daily standups and by keeping your stories to five days effort, you avoid the issues encountered when someone goes to work on something for several weeks, and resurfaces only for you to find that the work was done wrong or not needed.

- **Defects**: Pulling a resource to work on a defect interrupts the current work in progress of that resource. You reduce this effect by limiting the number of concurrent items being covered by a resource. You reduce the number of defects by reducing the lag between requirements gathering and build, and by more actively involving the customer in the project.

An idea for you to get your team involved in recognizing waste, is for you to build a simple, three column worksheet that you post in your project room, listing out the above sources of waste. The first column then is "Waste," second column is "Observed," and third is "Cause." You can ask team members to fill this out whenever they spot waste.

You can also hold brainstorming sessions to fill out this template.

Kanban does not formally call out the need for retrospectives. You saw in Scrum that the team holds a retrospective at the end of each sprint, to discuss what went right and what went wrong. Although Kanban does not specifically call these out, Kanban does tell you to focus on Kaizen, continuous improvement, and you will therefore want to schedule periodic retrospectives. At these meetings you can discuss items like waste, bottlenecks and blocks, to get the team's input on how you can improve your project processes.

Defect tracking

There are numerous approaches to managing defects. The key thing to remember in Kanban, is that the board must contain all work that a team is working on. Otherwise, you will not be able to manage WIP. On a typical SAP project, we use a third party, defect tracker to log and manage defects during integration testing. We then hold daily meetings to review, prioritize and assign defects. In Agile, we are continually integration testing throughout the projects. The management overhead for defects is removed, because the users are finding bugs "at the same time" that the work is being constructed. There is no longer a month, or several months delay, between when the configuration or development was completed, to when we find the defect.

Defects are high priority. A work item cannot be considered done until the defects related to it are closed. Given most defects will be discovered when the related work item is still on the board, then there is no need to create a separate work item for the defect. The tester simply informs the owner of the defect so that it can be fixed. The work item remains in the "testing" column until all related defects are resolved.

If a defect is discovered after a work item has been initially passed, then a separate work item will need to be created. This can occur during regression testing, when a larger subset of stories is being tested together, and a previously passed story fails a test. In this case, a new work item for the defect must be created. Ideally, we want work items to be at least one day of effort. If you have multiple, smaller defects, then tie them together into one work item. You will want to run most defects through your expediting lane, or flag them as critical, so that integration testing is not delayed.

A tracker may be useful for recording defect information, such as screenshots, and textual details about how to replicate the error. Recording this information will be important when saving low priority defects. Defects that get found after the story has been considered done, may need to be recorded in a tracker, so that screenshots and details can be captured. They must also get added to the backlog at the same time, so that they can be prioritized.

But always think about the pros and cons of a tracker in terms of overhead. Ultimately, if a tracker is used, it should be simply a tool at the disposal of the team, to be used only when deemed necessary by the tester. There must never be a rule that all defects must be logged in the tracker, because it can rarely be argued that there is true customer value to logging each and every defect. Since we have baked resolution of defects into our definition of done, and each story is completed on average in five days, then there is little argument for expecting the team to log those defects.

Keep in mind that if there are too many defects, a root cause analysis should be performed, to get to the underlying causes of the lower quality code or configuration. Perhaps the test cases themselves need to be improved.

How to manage new work

Just as in traditional projects, new work that is not yet in the backlog will get identified during the project. Just as in Scrum, the business owner will be responsible for prioritizing any new work. They will need to reprioritize the backlog, and ensure that the new work gets placed in the correct sequence. Kanban has a benefit over Scrum, in that the business owner does not need to wait until the next sprint before work can begin on a new work item. As soon as a free slot opens on the board, a new, high priority work item can be started.

The product owner can either swap out an existing equivalently sized item from the backlog, or remove lower priority items. If not, then you can expect an impact on the overall project schedule. Depending on the project charter, a formal change request may be required.

Visible policies

When first building your Kanban board, you need to agree on policies that will be used to manage the work. The above sections have shown you some of the items you will want to consider. These policies should be posted near the physical

Kanban board, or in an easily accessible public folder, if an electronic board is being used.

Some typical policies to consider are:

- Pull from the top of the input queue
- Track only work items of one hour of effort, or greater, on the board
- Work only on items that appear on the board (the board contains the full scope of project work and deliverables)
- Do not exceed the specified WIP limit
- Enter the start date and calculated due date based on the service level agreement for each new work item.

In addition to a separate policy, each lane on the board should have the pull criteria identified. For example, in order for a work item to be pulled into user acceptance testing, it must have been unit tested.

Project reporting

Most suggestions on project reporting have been embedded in this book in the section relevant to the topic. For example, burndown reports were covered in the section on Scrum, since they are typically only used in the Scrum approach. Similarly, throughput charts were discussed in the Kanban section, given they are typically used only in the Kanban approach. This section will discuss some additional reporting suggestions from the Agile experts that apply to both approaches.

Most Agile approaches shy away from complex project plans, simply because they are often so far removed from the reality of the project. I have discussed this elsewhere in the book, but really it comes to the fact that on a complex SAP project, it is nearly impossible to predict down to the detailed task level months out, with any level of true accuracy. Agile reminds us that the past is the best predictor of future performance. We need to get some work done before we can predict both what, and how much work, we can complete in the next cycle. However, you may not be able to avoid preparing and submitting reports using Gantts, and data from a project software, such as Microsoft® Project®.

Mike Cohn, in *Agile Estimating and Planning*, suggests that we create project plan elements for each story or feature. Do not load the technical tasks in the plan. This continues to keep the focus on deliverables that hold meaning to the customer. Roll the stories up to a release work breakdown structure element. This way you can communicate progress at the release level.

Another reporting suggestion from Mike Cohn is to use a parking lot chart. A parking lot chart simply consists of a table per theme that lists the total number of stories in the theme, followed by a percentage, indicating the percent of completed stories for that theme. You can add a progress bar to show a better visual indicator. Adapting this to SAP, your Business Process Map process steps should serve as your themes. Create one box per process step, and use that to report on the amount of completed stories.

CHAPTER 6: FINAL PREPARATION

In the standard ASAP methodology, the purpose of final preparation is to finalize business preparedness, deliver training, prepare for the transition to production support and perform cutover. In Agile, the purpose and deliverables remain the same, with the difference being that we run final preparation for each release. In essence then, each release is a mini project. As part of each production release, the training documents and course schedule must be in place. A business readiness plan, including job restructuring needs, should have been completed, or be in the process of being completed. Your sustainment organization needs to be in place, and you will need to prepare all required handover documents for operations and sustainment. A preliminary cutover plan should be in place, as you will now perform cutover rehearsal, and actual cutover, if releasing to production.

The amount of time you plan for the final preparation activities will depend on the complexity and size of the build of your release. Having been on numerous projects, the one thing that can be said, is that there is no magic formula to calculate the schedule for final preparation activities. We typically overlap many of these activities with the final integration test activities from realization. For example, cutover rehearsals will typically be run in tandem with integration testing. Training delivery will often begin during the final cycle of integration testing.

Much of the need to overlap activities on a traditional project comes from lateness having been passed down the schedule. This lateness forces the project to squeeze the final preparation activities into a smaller window, to meet a go live constraint. The benefit of the Agile approach to using releases, is that the volume of work during project preparation will have been greatly reduced. It is important that you schedule an iteration to run final preparation. This could mean a one month iteration, or a two week iteration, depending on the size and complexity of the release. By involving the entire team in cutover rehearsals, you will spread the workload, reduce the duration, and bring the entire team's knowledge to the cutover effort.

The training, organization change management, cutover planning and production readiness activities, are activities that need to be started during realization. These activities should not have been assigned to the core team. The core team needs to have been free to complete the core solution deliverables. This means that just as in a traditional project, there will be some overhead for resources devoted to preparing the organization for go live.

If you are only releasing to the quality environment in this release, then you should still run through the cutover rehearsals, in order to acquire the knowledge needed to perform actual cutover, and to reduce the effort required for the actual cutover. You want to obtain the benefit of having divided the larger project into releases. If you avoid cutover rehearsals in a release to the quality environment, then you will be left with a large cutover activity when you release to production. There is much benefit to be gained by having the team rehearse go live. They can better prepare for final cutover and thereby reduce go live risk. They can also prepare detailed cutover plans that can be leveraged in the next cutover.

If a mid project release cuts over to production, your project will be running in parallel with the sustainment stabilization and support. You will need to carefully manage this transition, to ensure a minimal pull on your project from the sustainment organization. The potential risk of needing project support for sustainment, will have been reduced by the increase in integration testing that occurred during your Agile approach. Through continued integration testing, you will find that the quality of the system has been greatly improved, and the risk of major defects being found by sustainment, is reduced. Members from your sustainment team should have been involved in testing, and therefore understand the business process and system. The sustainment team will be in a much stronger position to more independently support the solution.

Following final preparation, your team returns to the activities of the next release.

APPENDIX A: DEVELOPMENT APPROACH

It's important to discuss the differences in Agile as it pertains to the project's development approach.

Traditionally, functional specifications are prepared for each RICEFW object by the appropriate analyst. This is then formally reviewed prior to being handed off to the developer. The developer then writes a technical specification. This is also normally reviewed. The next step is to code the entire object. Following initial code, the developer will perform technical unit testing of the object. The developer then submits the object for functional unit testing by the analyst. The analyst tests the object, according to a set of unit tests that they defined. Defects are raised and corrected until the object passes functional unit testing. At that time the object is "filed away" for a few months until integration testing begins.

This process is very heavy, and takes a considerable amount of time. In Agile, we want to break the object into smaller pieces. For example, an interface from a time system to CAT2 can be broken down first into enough code to mock up a file and send a small set of data to CAT2. A second story might involve writing the code to read a file, or enable an enterprise service, depending on whether the interface is batch or real time. Subsequent pieces of code are added through additional stories, until the full story is complete.

The code is not based on a specification unless absolutely necessary. Instead, the initial acceptance tests identified during blueprint are expanded on in a test case document. As an example, a test might state "when executing this interface, the output file will contain the following fields." Another test might read "test that field x is the sum of the following wage types." This approach dramatically reduces the development turnaround time, since the test case is used both as specification and test document. Additional artifacts, such as mappings and translations, can be added to supplement the tests. The benefit of tests is that they will be kept up to date, whereas a specification is typically old by the time the project reaches go live.

The RICEFW stories must be scheduled near to the time when their related configuration is being worked on. This will ensure that the configuration takes the RICEFW requirements into consideration, and that the developer better understands the configuration. In the best case, the developer and configurator will analyze the requirements, and design for both configuration and RICEFW as a team.

Processes that do not add value to the customer should be removed. Sign offs rarely add value. Reviews are important in some cases. Review each case independently. Use value stream mapping to review your development process. This will help you identify the activities that take up considerable time, but add little value.

Do not code features that are not needed "today." Do not build in things that you "think" will be needed eventually, some time post go live. This will reduce work effort and keep the team focused on delivering the value that the project was designed to deliver.

Do not attempt to have the perfect design before coding. The Poppendiecks discuss the importance of concurrent development and having rapid "try it, test it, fix it" cycles (*Lean Software Development: An Agile Toolkit*). Concurrent development means starting code as soon as an initial design is ready. This leaves room for knowledge and experimentation, and getting it right. This means that instead of adding more documentation or detailed planning, your developers should try out ideas by iteratively cycling through requirements, design and code for a given story.

The Poppendiecks argue that sequential development attempts to be too "predictive." Sequential development is when we attempt to define all requirements, and design for a given object prior to coding. This requires the developer to commit, upfront, to initial design decisions, and complete the object based on those initial assumptions. If the developer finds an error in the design, they are typically so far into the process that it is too costly to go back and redesign. Concurrent development allows you to adjust more quickly, and adapt to final decisions. The goal is to postpone decisions to the last possible moment, so that you do not get locked in to them.

Concurrent development does require more senior developers, as they need to be able to anticipate where a design is heading as it is played out. This can also be managed by having a complement of lead developers who work with the less experienced members to guide the concurrent development process.

FURTHER RESOURCES

Books

Agile Estimating and Planning, Cohn, M, Prentice Hall, 1 edition (Nov 11 2005), ISBN 978-0131479418.

Agile Management for Software Engineering: Applying the Theory of Constraints for Business Results, Anderson, D, Prentice Hall, 1 edition (Sep 27 2003), ISBN 978-0131424609.

Agile Software Development Evaluating the Methods for Your Organization, Koch, A, Artech House Publishers, 1 edition (Nov 5 2004), ISBN 978-1580538428.

Agile Software Development with Scrum, Schwaber, K and Beedle, M, Prentice Hall, 1 edition (Oct 21 2001), ISBN 978-0130676344.

Agile testing: A Practical Guide for Testers and Agile Teams, Crispin, Lisa, and Gregory, Janet, Addison-Wesley Professional, 1 edition (Jan 9 2009), ISBN: 978-0321534460.

Kanban: Successful Evolutionary Change for Your Technology Business, Anderson, D, Blue Hole Press (2010), ISBN 978-0984521401.

Lean Software Development: An Agile Toolkit, Poppendieck, M and Poppendieck, T, Addison-Wesley Professional, 1 edition (May 18 2003), ISBN 978-0321150783.

Further Resources

Succeeding With Agile: Software Development Using Scrum, Cohn, Mike, Addison-Wesley Professional, 1 edition (Nov 5 2009), ISBN 978-0321579362.

The Toyota Way: 14 Management Principles from the World's Greatest Manufacturer, Liker, Jeffrey, McGraw-Hill, 1 edition (Dec 17 2003), ISBN 978-0071392310.

User Stories Applied: For Agile Software Development, Cohn, M, Addison-Wesley Professional, 1 edition (Mar 11 2004), ISBN 978-0321205681.

User Story Mapping, Patton, Jeff, O'Reilly Media, 1 edition (March 22 2013), ISBN 978-1449304553.

Websites

SAP best practices

help.sap.com/bestpractices

Scrum overview

www.jeffsutherland.com/scrumhandbook.pdf

Dependency diagrams

http://it.toolbox.com/blogs/enterprise-solutions/using-dependency-diagrams-16512

Agile ASAP methodology add on

http://scn.sap.com/community/asap-methodology/blog/2011/05/11/asap-goes-agile

Silent planning poker

http://systemagility.com/?s=silent+grouping

Further Resources

Solution demos

http://scn.sap.com/community/asap-methodology/blog/2010/07/07/implementation-acceleration-techniques--beyond-Agile-methods

SAP test driven development (requires SAP passport)

http://scn.sap.com/docs/DOC-10310

SAP IDES systems

http://wiki.sdn.sap.com/wiki/display/HOME/IDES

Agile manifesto

www.agilemanifesto.org/

Kanban games

www.shmula.com/paper-airplane-game-pull-systems-push-systems/8280/

Acceptance tests

www.scrumalliance.org/articles/414-an-argument-for-comprehensive-user-stories

Agile contracts

www.mountaingoatsoftware.com/presentations/planning-for-contract-agile-projects

Story mapping

www.agileproductdesign.com/blog/the_new_backlog.html

Slicing

www.agileproductdesign.com/writing/how_you_slice_it.pdf

Further Resources

Planning poker

www.renaissancesoftware.net/

XP

http://xprogramming.com/book/whatisxp/

ITG RESOURCES

IT Governance Ltd sources, creates and delivers products and services to meet the real-world, evolving IT governance needs of today's organisations, directors, managers and practitioners.

The ITG website (*www.itgovernance.co.uk*) is the international one-stop-shop for corporate and IT governance information, advice, guidance, books, tools, training and consultancy.

www.itgovernance.co.uk/project_governance.aspx is the information page on our website for Agile resources.

Other Websites

Books and tools published by IT Governance Publishing (ITGP) are available from all business booksellers and are also immediately available from the following websites:

www.itgovernance.eu is our euro-denominated website which ships from Benelux and has a growing range of books in European languages other than English.

www.itgovernanceusa.com is a US$-based website that delivers the full range of IT Governance products to North America, and ships from within the continental US.

www.itgovernanceasia.com provides a selected range of ITGP products specifically for customers in the Indian sub-continent.

www.itgovernance.asia delivers the full range of ITGP publications, serving countries across Asia Pacific. Shipping from Hong Kong, US dollars, Singapore dollars, Hong Kong dollars, New Zealand dollars and Thai baht are all accepted through the website.

www.27001.com is the IT Governance Ltd website that deals specifically with information security management, and ships from within the continental US.

Toolkits

ITG's unique range of toolkits includes the IT Governance Framework Toolkit, which contains all the tools and guidance that you will need in order to develop and implement an appropriate IT governance framework for your organisation. Full details can be found at *www.itgovernance.co.uk/products/519*.

For a free paper on how to use the proprietary Calder-Moir IT Governance Framework, and for a free trial version of the toolkit, see *www.itgovernance.co.uk/calder_moir.aspx*.

There is also a wide range of toolkits to simplify implementation of management systems, such as an ISO/IEC 27001 ISMS or an ISO/IEC 22301 BCMS, and these can all be viewed and purchased online at: *www.itgovernance.co.uk*.

Training Services

IT Governance offers an extensive portfolio of training courses designed to educate information security, IT governance, risk management and compliance professionals. Our classroom and online training programmes will help you develop the skills required to deliver best practice and compliance for your organisation. They will also enhance your career by providing you with industry-standard certifications and increased peer recognition. Our range of courses offers a structured learning path from foundation to advanced level in the key topics of information security, IT governance, business continuity and IT service management.

Full details of all IT Governance training courses can be found at *www.itgovernance.co.uk/training.aspx*.

Professional Services and Consultancy

The IT Governance Professional Services team can show you how to apply Agile concepts to the most complex SAP projects. Our expert consultants can guide and inspire you in the use of Agile, providing you with the practical techniques to improve delivery efficiencies, control your implementation costs and, meet your sales targets by building long-term customer loyalty.

We can mentor and coach you in Agile methods, improving your project's flexibility, transparency and speed, and enabling you to adapt to any changes more readily and effectively. We can also guide you in ways that allow you to appropriately involve internal and external customers throughout the duration of your project.

Our detailed advice, based on years of Agile project experience, will help to ensure that you meet the objectives of your contractual obligations.

For more information about IT Governance: Consultancy and Training Services see *www.itgovernance.co.uk/consulting.aspx*.

Publishing Services

IT Governance Publishing (ITGP) is the world's leading IT-GRC publishing imprint that is wholly owned by IT Governance Ltd.

With books and tools covering all IT governance, risk and compliance frameworks, we are the publisher of choice for authors and distributors alike, producing unique and practical publications of the highest quality, in the latest formats available, which readers will find invaluable.

www.itgovernancepublishing.co.uk is the website dedicated to ITGP, enabling both current and future authors, distributors, readers and other interested parties, to have easier access to more information allowing them to keep up to date with the latest publications and news from ITGP.

Newsletter

IT governance is one of the hottest topics in business today, not least because it is also the fastest moving.

You can stay up to date with the latest developments across the whole spectrum of IT governance subject matter, including risk management, information security, ITIL and IT service management, project governance, compliance and so much more, by subscribing to ITG's core publications and topic alert emails.

Simply visit our subscription centre and select your preferences: *www.itgovernance.co.uk/newsletter.aspx*.